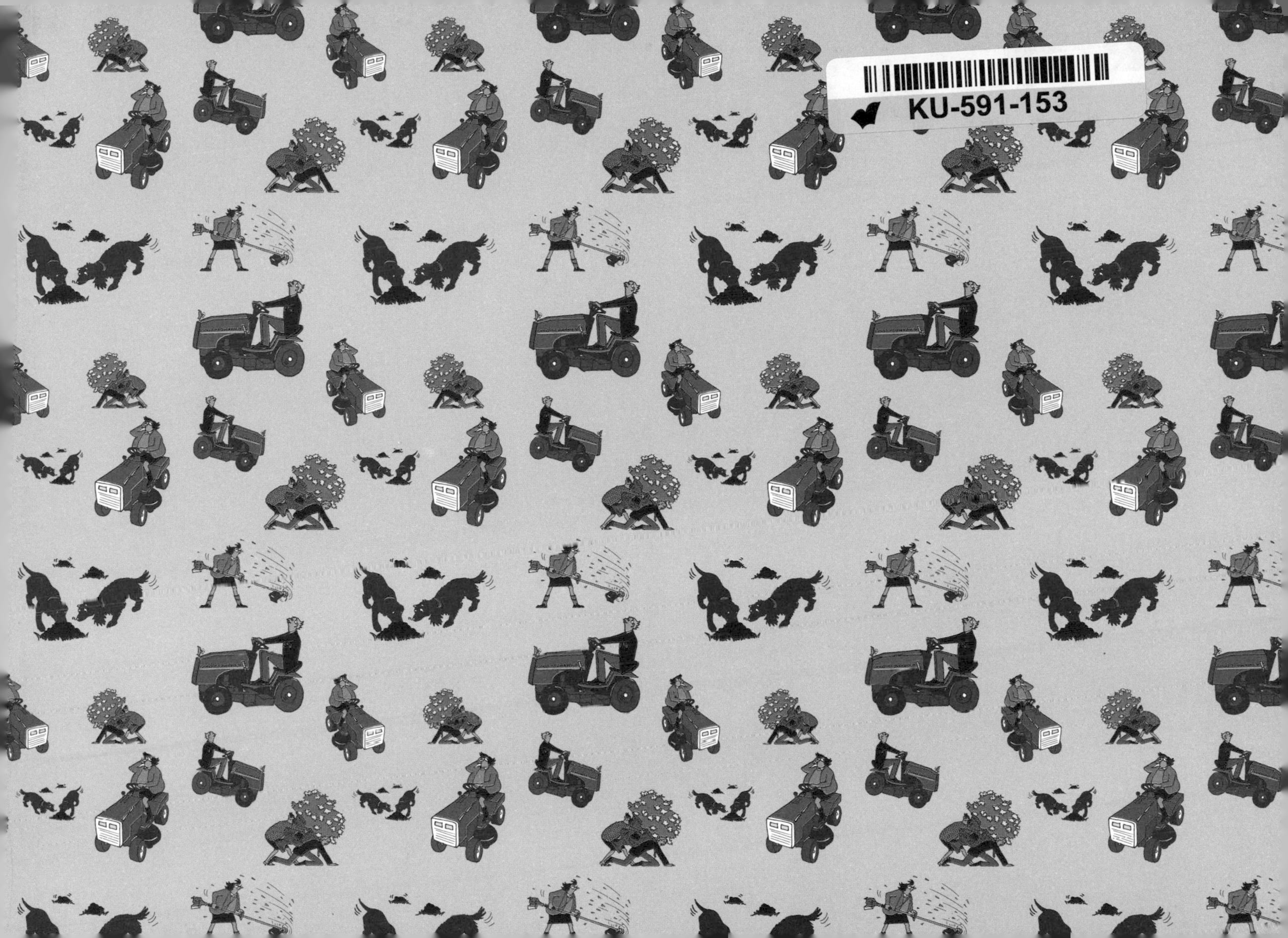

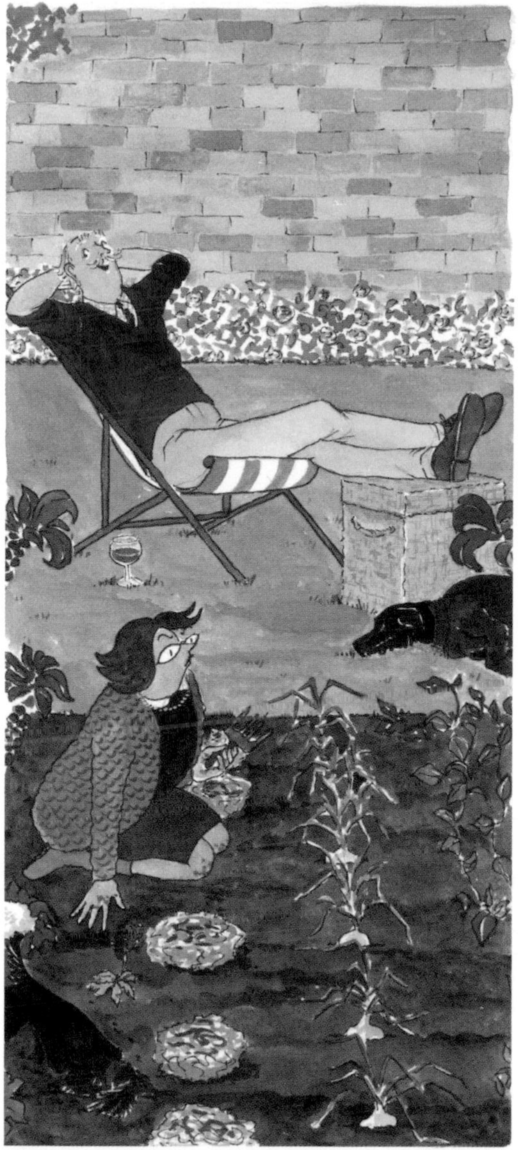

TOTTERING-BY-GENTLY®

In the Garden with THE TOTTERINGS

ANNIE TEMPEST

Quiller

First published in the UK in 2011 by Frances Lincoln Ltd

This revised edition published in 2019 by Quiller,
an imprint of Amberley Publishing

British Library Cataloguing-in-Publication Data
A catalogue record for this book is available from the
British Library.

ISBN 978 1 84689 3001

Printed in China

Quiller
An imprint of Amberley Publishing
The Hill,Merrywalks, Stroud GL5 4EP
Tel: 01453 847800
Email: info@quillerbooks.com
Website: www.quillerpublishing.com

Other books by Annie Tempest

Drinks with the Totterings *Tails of Tottering Hall*
The Totterings' Desk Diary *She Talks Venus / He talks Mars*
The Totterings' Pocket Diary *Lord Tottering: An English Gentleman*
Tottering-by-Gently Annual *Out and About with the Totterings*
At Home with the Totterings *Tottering-by-Gently – First 20 years*
Tottering Life *Tottering-by-Gently Vols I, II and III*
The Tottering Journal *Becoming an English Squire*

THE TOTTERING-BY-GENTLY ROSE

This bee-friendly English shrub rose
was launched by David Austin Roses
at the RHS Chelsea Flower Show 2018
to celebrate the 25th Anniversary of
Tottering-by-Gently by Annie Tempest.

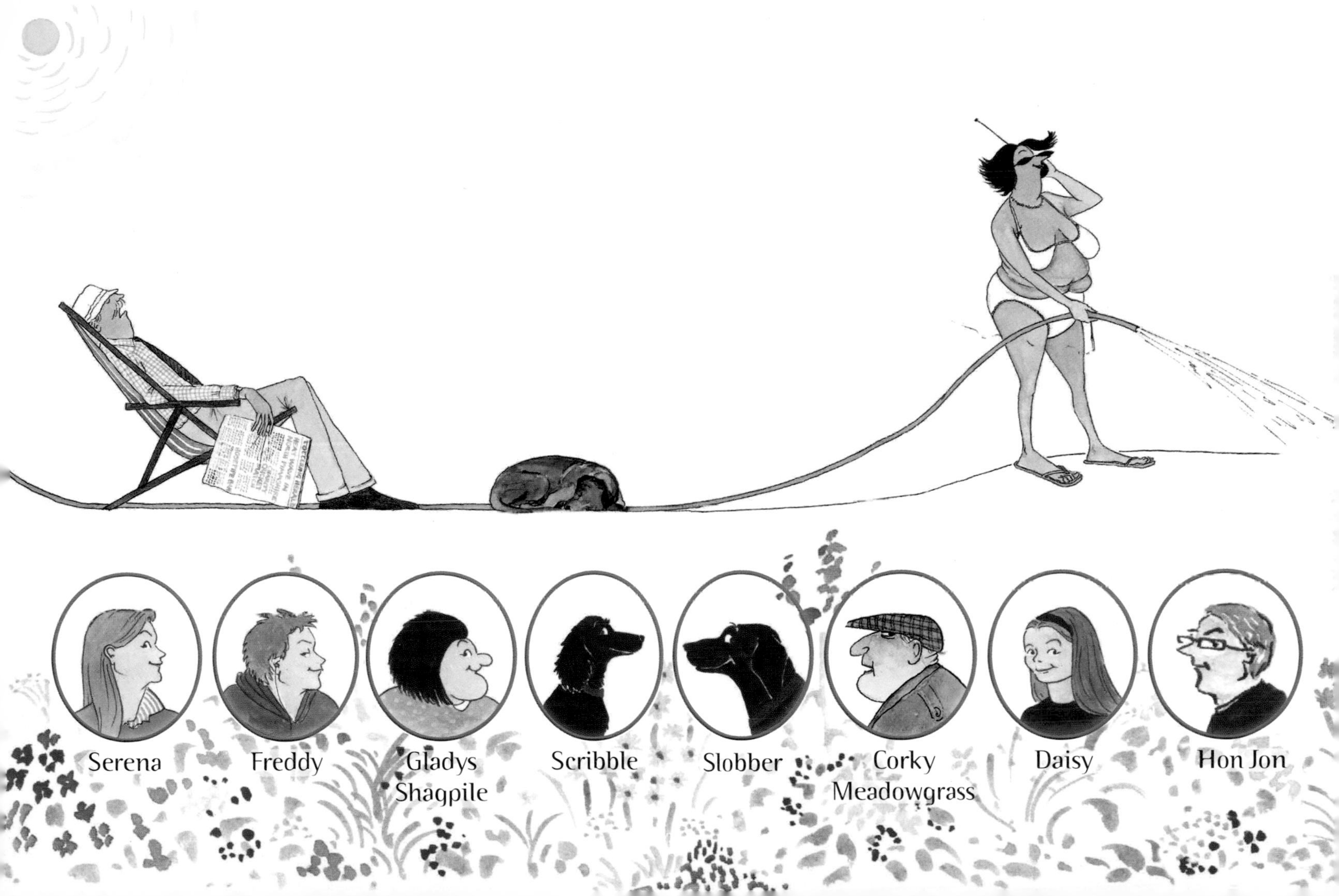
Serena
Freddy
Gladys Shagpile
Scribble
Slobber
Corky Meadowgrass
Daisy
Hon Jon

THE TOTTERING STORY

Tottering-by-Gently® is the creation of Annie Tempest and has run as a cartoon strip in *Country Life* magazine since 6th January, 1994.

Raymond O'Shea of The O'Shea Gallery, formerly of St. James's London, became Annie's agent and mentor in 1996. Between them, over the past 25 years, they have worked as a formidable team to turn Tottering-by-Gently® into one of the best known brands in the British cartoon world.

Daffy Tottering is a woman of a certain age who has been taken into the hearts of people all over the world. She reflects the daily challenges of modern life and has a pragmatic, wry wisdom commenting on universal subjects such as dieting, gardening, health and technology.

To view the ever increasing range of Tottering-by-Gently® products including champagne, wine, gin, jigsaws, books, diaries, calendars, greeting cards, mugs, postcards, prints, table mats, aprons and other textiles, visit www.tottering.com or email enquiries to daffy@tottering.com

TOTTERING AND QUILLER

Following the sell-out of the previous Tottering titles, we are delighted to form a new publishing relationship with Quiller Publishing. '*In the Garden with THE TOTTERINGS*' is the first in a series of books, some completely new and some re-issues of great favourites with additions of recent work.

THE TOTTERING STUDIOS

Annie's studio and gallery are located in North Norfolk where all the original watercolours are on display. For information on original drawing sales, commissions or gallery and studio visits, please contact: Raymond O'Shea at lordtottering@hotmail.com

ANNIE TEMPEST

Annie Tempest was born in 1959 in Lusaka, Zambia to the second son of a landed Yorkshire family. In 1972, her father's elder brother died and her father, the spare to the heir, inherited the estate and moved the family to the crumbling stately home of Broughton Hall. The Hall was then dry-rot ridden and leaking and was said to be too wet to burn down and tadpoles came out of the taps.

Annie started out in the world of cartooning in the *Daily Express*, with a daily pocket cartoon called WestEnders. She soon moved across to the rival *Daily Mail* where her timely cartoon strip 'The Yuppies' ran for seven and a half years and won her 'Strip Cartoonist of the year' in 1989.

As Annie's career as a cartoonist developed, she decided to draw on her childhood memories of the freezing northern pile for inspiration and so embarked on her award-winning Tottering-by-Gently strip which has run in *Country Life* for more than 25 years now. In 2009, this strip won her the prestigious Pont Prize for her portrayal of the British Character. Many of the interiors, furniture and paintings in her artwork are recognisable as from the now completely refurbished and centrally heated Hall in Annie's brother's guardianship today.

Although humour and illustration have always been Annie's first love, her drive to learn swept her into another arena – sculpting. For the past 15 years Annie has studied anatomy and sculpture, specialising in the human form and had a sell-out solo show at The O'Shea Gallery, London in 2012. She continues to divide her time between the two disciplines, along with producing Tottering-by-Gently fabrics and wall papers.

Annie lives with her dog, Dawa, in Norfolk.

FOREWORD

Lord and Lady Tottering have been friends of mine for years. I follow their exploits – domestic and horticultural – in *Country Life* every week, marvelling at the accuracy of their creator's ingenuity and her ability to hit the nail on the head when it comes to the joys, the delights and the frustrations of gardening.

Great columnists have the ability to articulate what their readers feel but cannot always put into words. Annie Tempest is similarly gifted when it comes to encapsulating a particular scenario and turning it from what could be nothing more than a trite observation into something that makes us smile at our own shortcomings. The trials and tribulations of the gardener are given a sense of perspective thanks to a deftness of brush-stroke and well-chosen words.

Annie understands the lines of demarcation that are frequently drawn between husband and wife on their shared piece of cultivated earth (she the creative one; he the labourer) and those garden features that are 'in' (smartly clipped topiary) and 'out' (hanging baskets). She knows the difference between a tuber and a rhizome. She also points out those things that we are sometimes reluctant to admit about ourselves – the jobs we avoid at all costs, and the constant exasperating war against weeds and pests – in spite of the fact that we persist in our laudable aim of being evangelically organic.

In Lady Tottering we have a British version of the Countess Von Arnim, who famously remarked: 'The best way to enjoy a garden is to put on a wide straw hat, hold a trowel in one hand and a gin and tonic in the other and tell the man where to dig. 'Except that Daffy – Lady T – is a little more hands on, and it is Dicky – Lord T – who nods indulgently at her handiwork when he brings out the life-saving G&T at that vital moment in late afternoon, which those of us who worry about our daily 'stiffener' like to call 'early evening'.

We all know a Lord and Lady Tottering and we can hear their voices quite clearly. We can see that green quilted jacket and tweed skirt bearing down on us when we visit an NGS garden, and tremble at the quizzical look bestowed upon us from behind the 'Dame Edna' glasses. We know ladies who are shaped like Daffy, and old colonels who are the spit of Dicky, and perhaps that is their greatest attribute – we recognise, if not ourselves, then people whom we know or have met.

Their names may be fictional, but their characters are drawn from life – sometimes a little too finely drawn for comfort (I am thinking of their anatomy in particular). It is for all these reasons that we love them and that we admire the woman who has brought Lord and Lady Tottering to life.

You need a sense of humour to be a gardener. Annie Tempest has it in spades.

Oh dear...I'm so sorry!

Alan Titchmarsh

GREAT GARDENING MOMENTS...

... That mug of Earl Grey next to a barrow full of couch grass

The Pleasure of Gardening

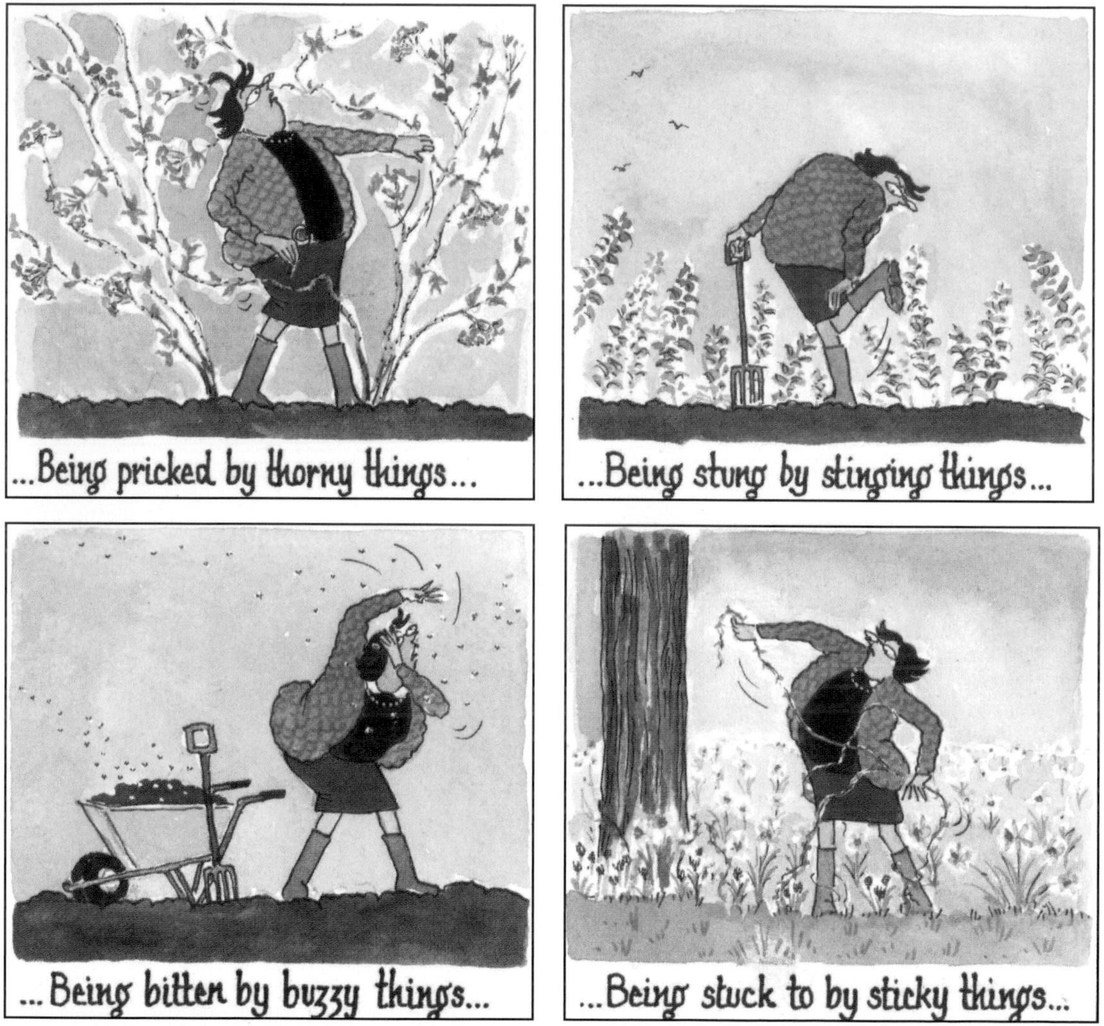
...Being pricked by thorny things...
...Being stung by stinging things...
...Being bitten by buzzy things...
...Being stuck to by sticky things...

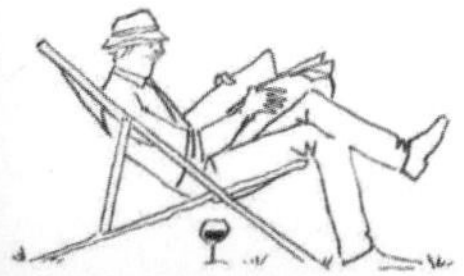

THE PERFECT MARRIAGE

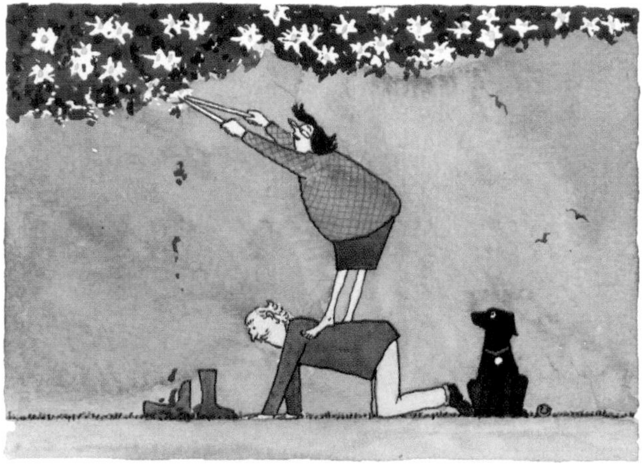

Being supportive ...

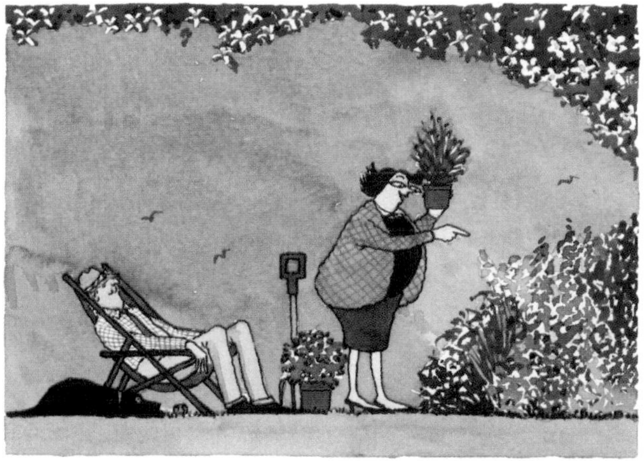

making time to listen to each other ...

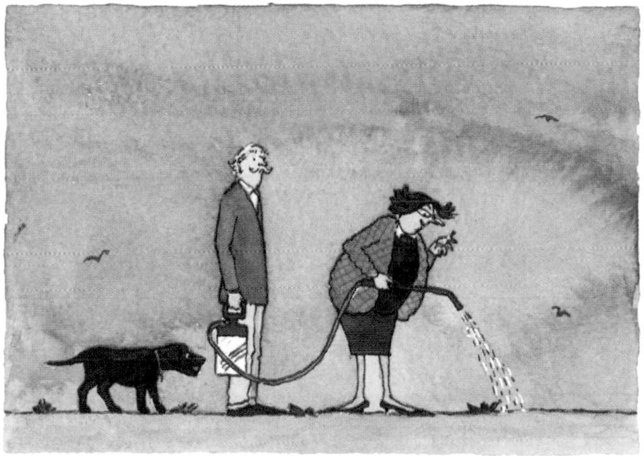

dealing with problems together ...

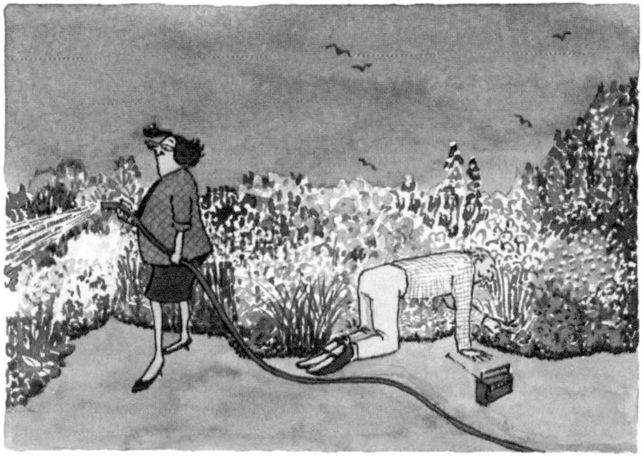

keeping active in the bed department ...

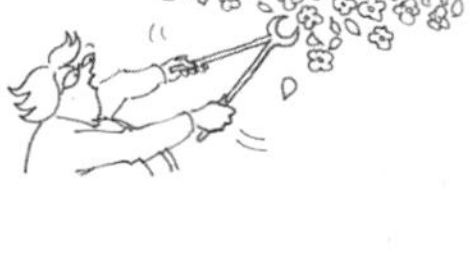

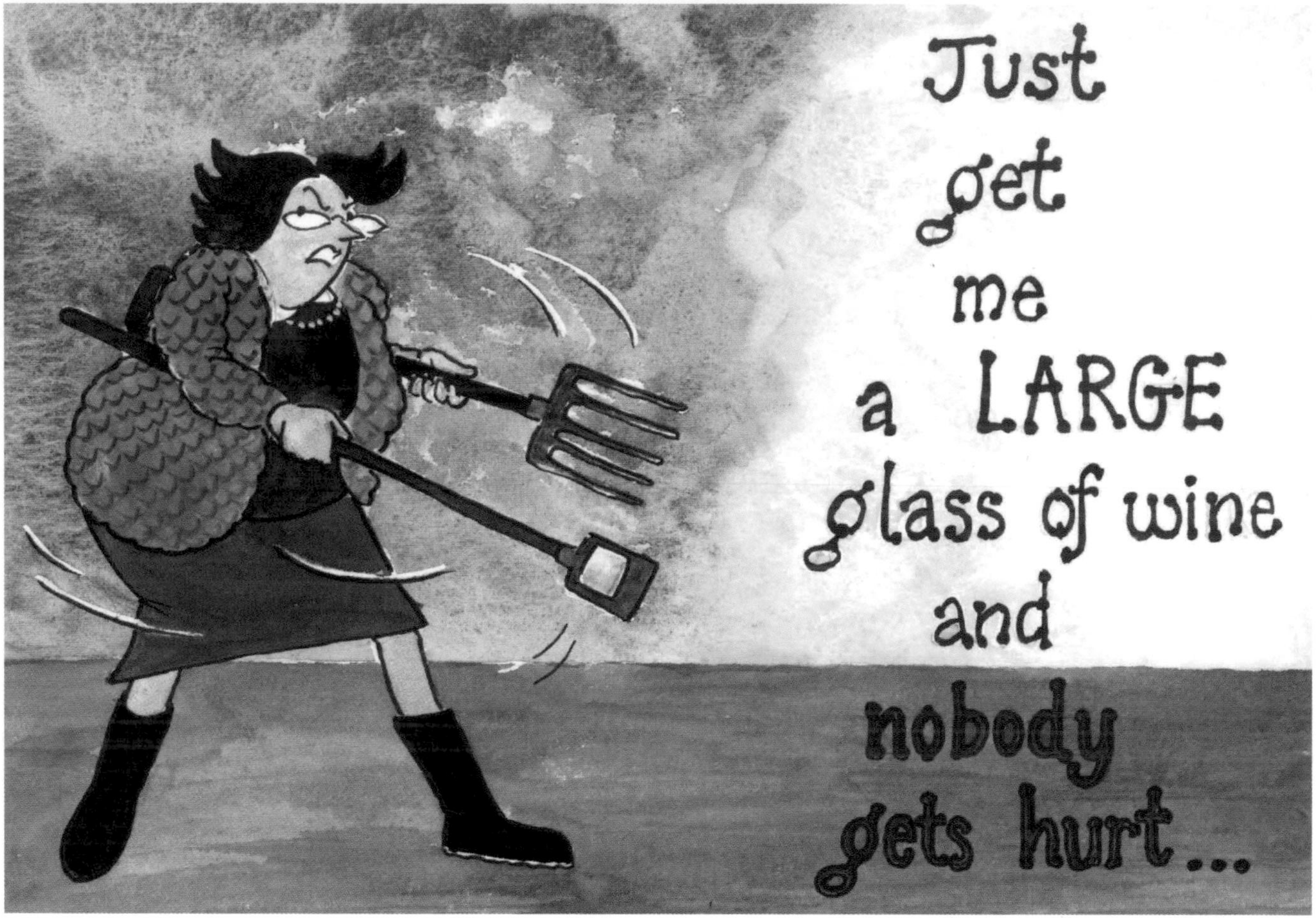
Just
get
me
a LARGE
glass of wine
and
nobody
gets hurt...

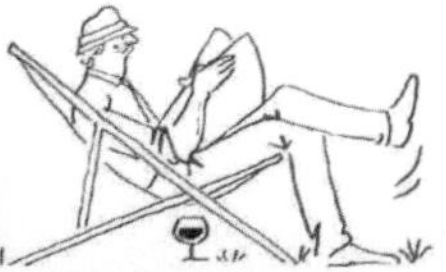

Marvellous natural remedy! She says it beats HRT hands down...

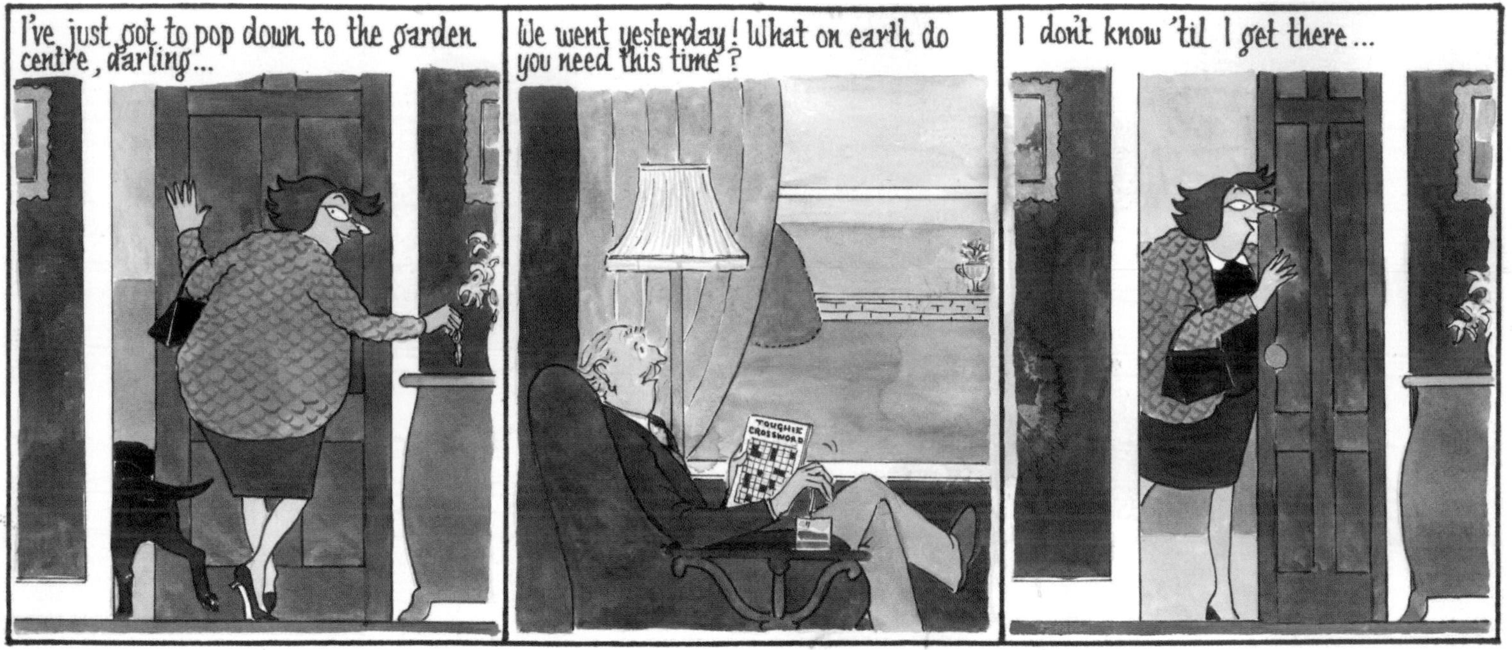

I've just got to pop down to the garden centre, darling...
We went yesterday! What on earth do you need this time?
TOUGHIE CROSSWORD
I don't know 'til I get there...

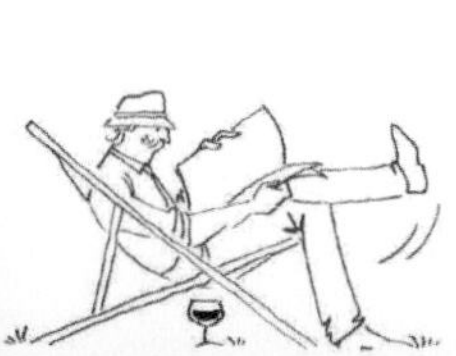

No, no – tell me, darling – you know I'm always dying to hear all about what ever you've been up to in the garden…

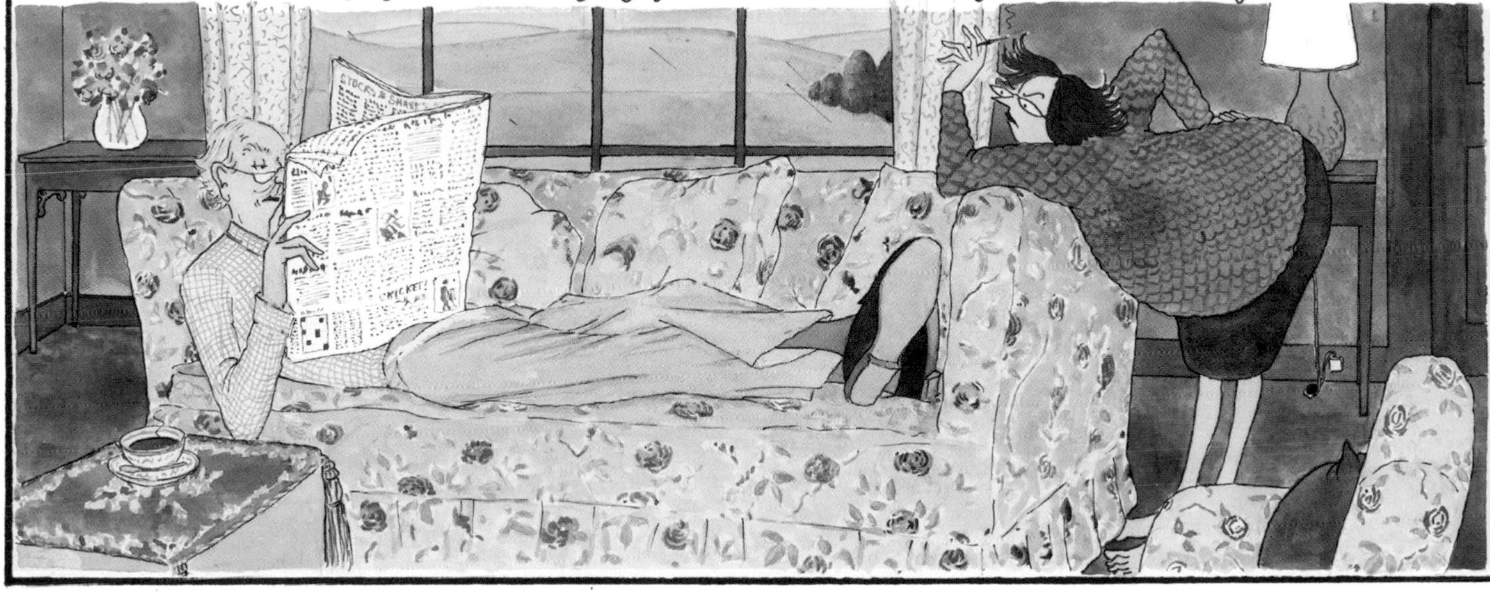

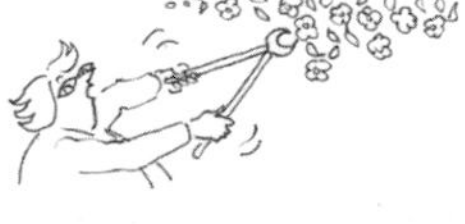

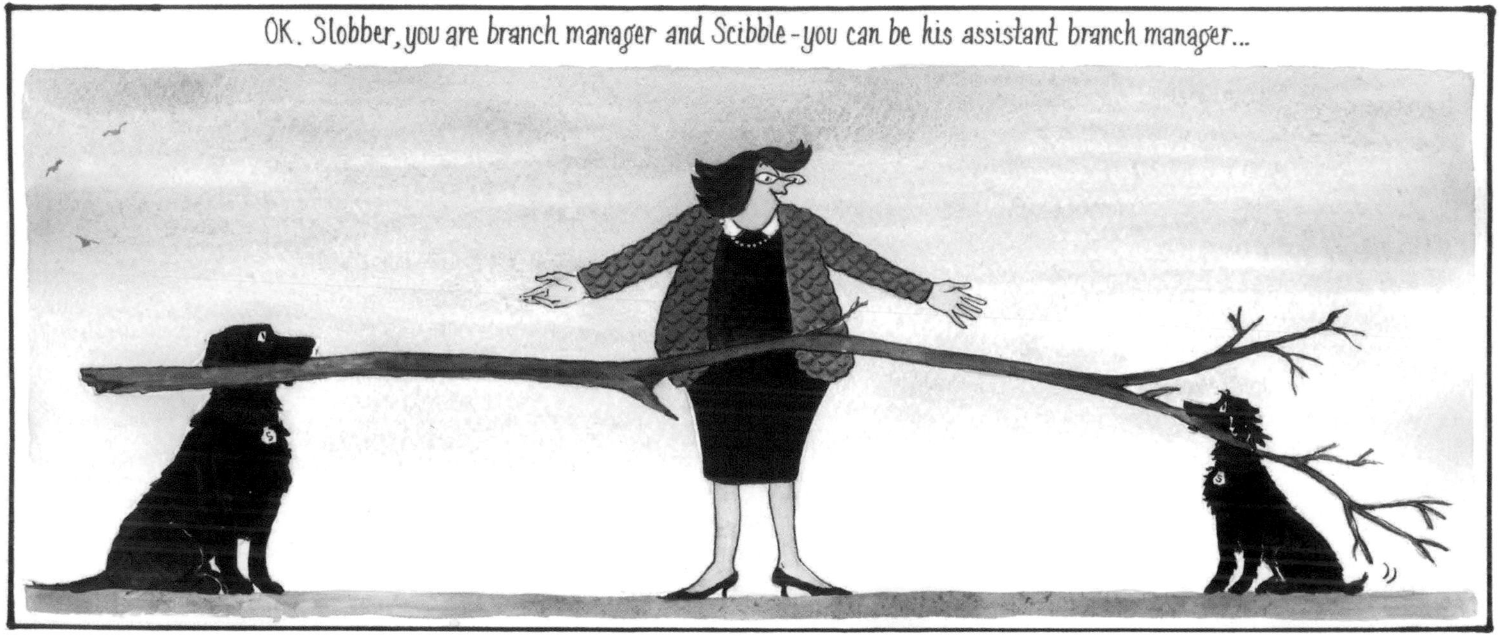
OK. Slobber, you are branch manager and Scibble - you can be his assistant branch manager...

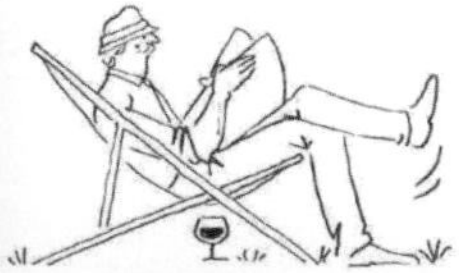

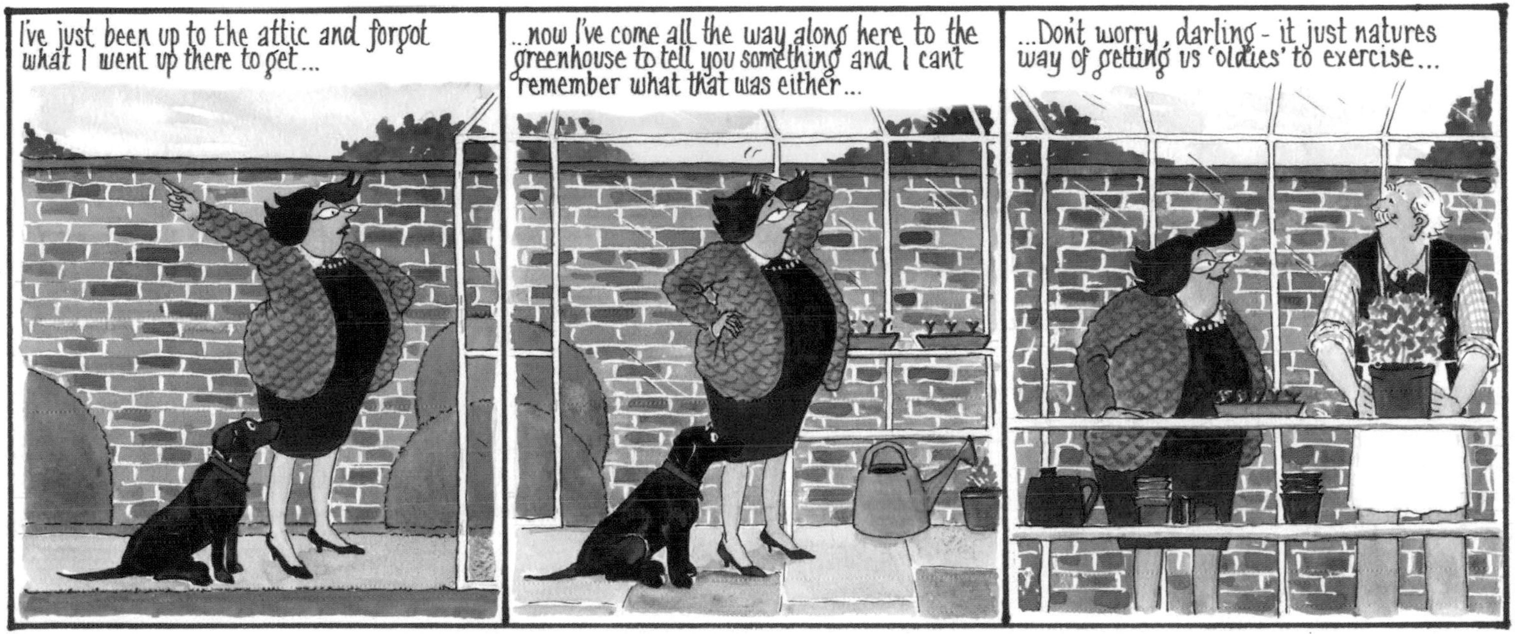
I've just been up to the attic and forgot what I went up there to get...
...now I've come all the way along here to the greenhouse to tell you something and I can't remember what that was either...
...Don't worry, darling - it just natures way of getting us 'oldies' to exercise...

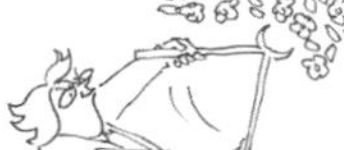

The young voted on the single issue of university tuition fees and ...
RING RING
SLUG Pellets
Excuse me, Daffy... I'll have to take this call...
RING RING!
SLUG Pellets
...it's our socialist granddaughter who can't make up her mind whether to go to Provence or stay for a 21st dance at The Hurlingham next week...
SLUG Pellets

I can't remember who but someone told me recently that Ginseng was good for the memory...

It took me months to remember to buy some...

...and I must have put it somewhere safe because I can't find it anywhere.

EVEN GARDENERS NEED TO TAKE TIME OUT...

...to smell the roses...

I'd like a pair of professional grade dog nail clippers, please.
VETERINA
RECEPTIC
Is this for Slobber Tottering? Would he prefer red or blue?
ROTTINGBEAM VETERINARIANS
THE PRACTICE THAT CALLS A SPAYED A SPAYED
He won't care. They're for pruning the crabapple tree...
VETERINAR
RECEPTIOI

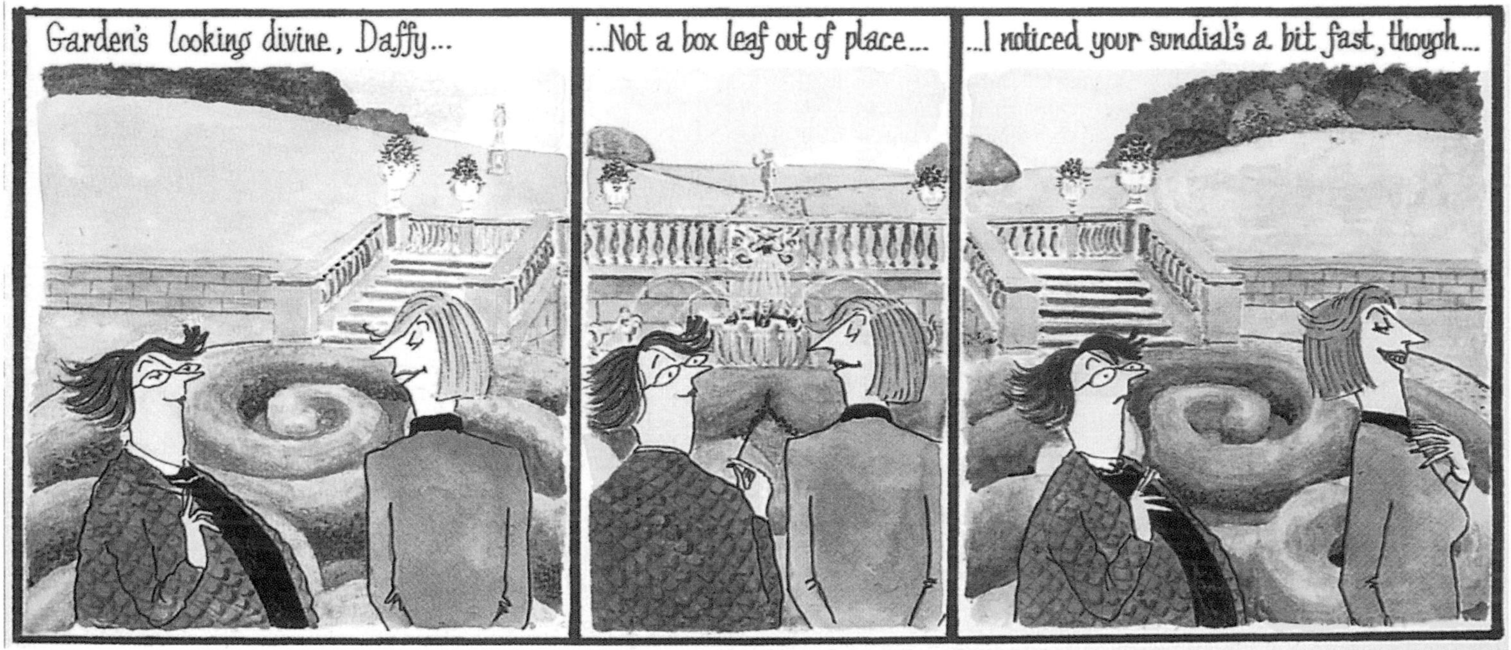
Garden's looking divine, Daffy...
...Not a box leaf out of place...
...I noticed your sundial's a bit fast, though...

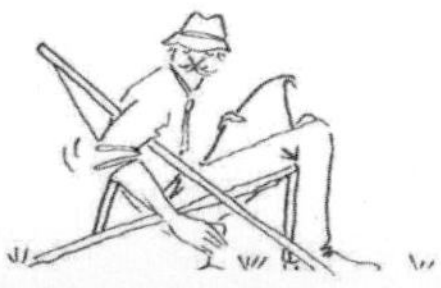

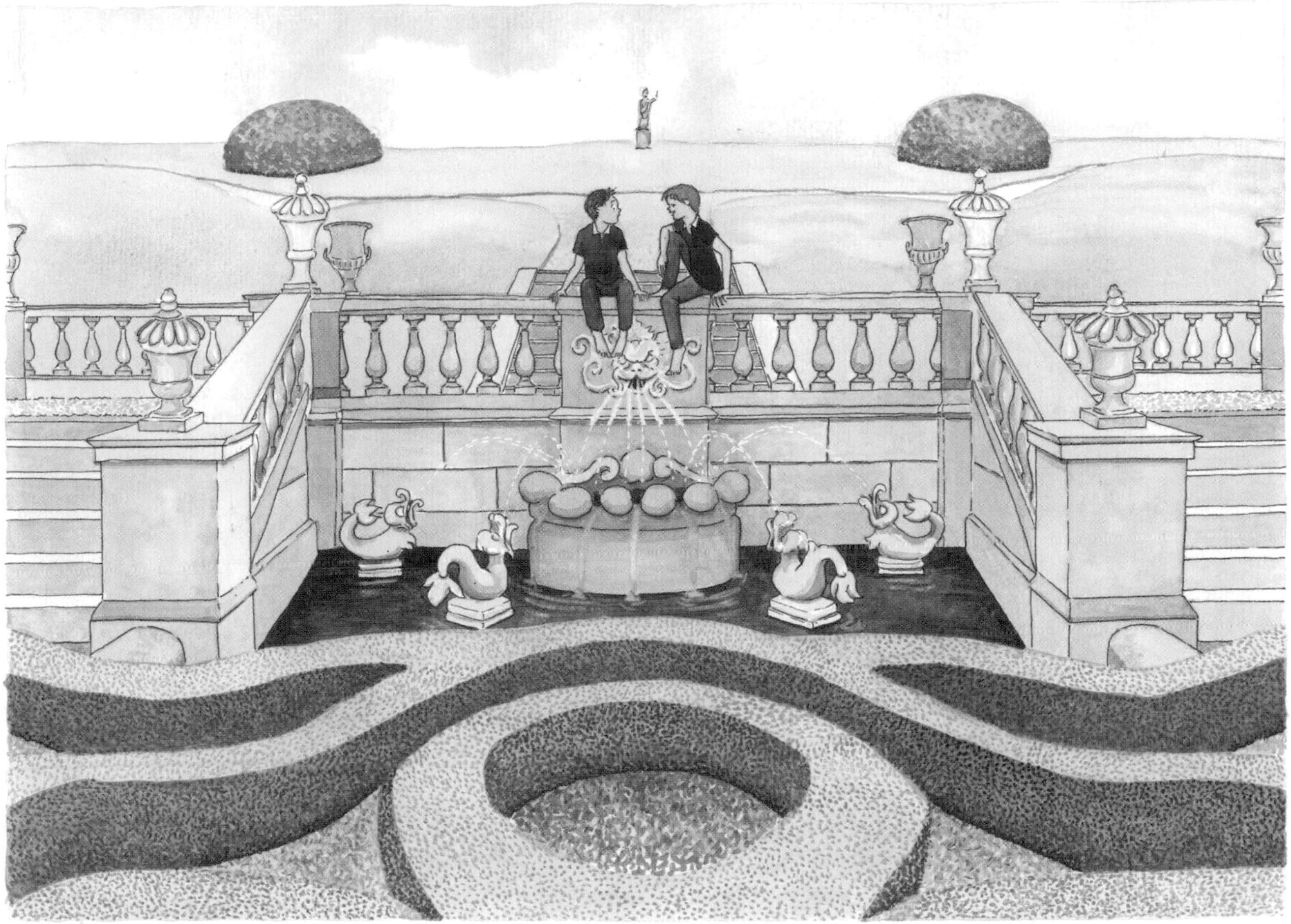

"If I haven't made a million by eighteen, then I'll just have to go into something my parents approve of..."

One's gardener weeding...   One's self weeding...

Just enjoy your Rosé on a sunny evening and focus on the flowers rather than on all the weeding you've got to do...

I know! Pretend I'm a friend and you're here strolling around _my_ garden...

You've got a nettle problem in your peonys...

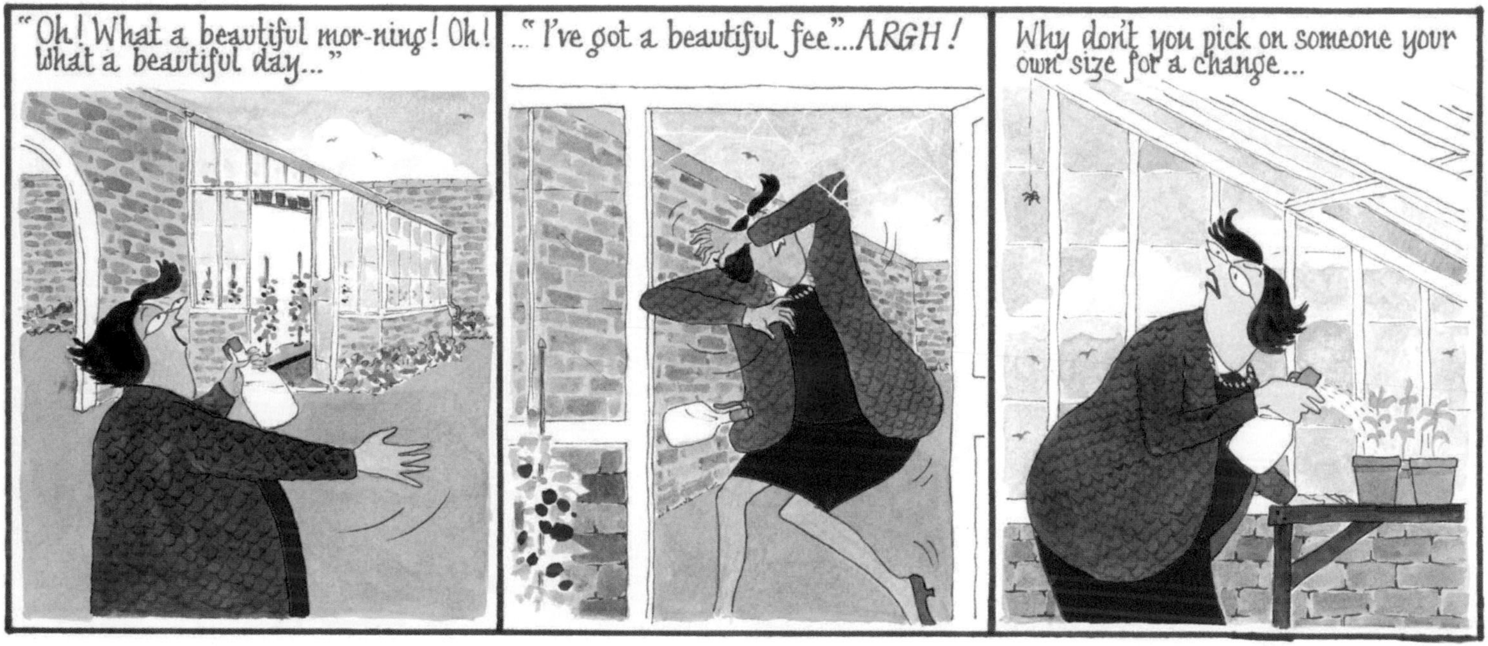
"Oh! What a beautiful mor-ning! Oh! What a beautiful day..."
..." I've got a beautiful fee"...ARGH!
Why don't you pick on someone your own size for a change...

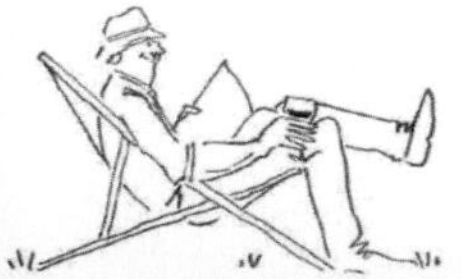

LADY TOTTERING at ORVIS in her 'SWISS ARMY BARBOUR'...

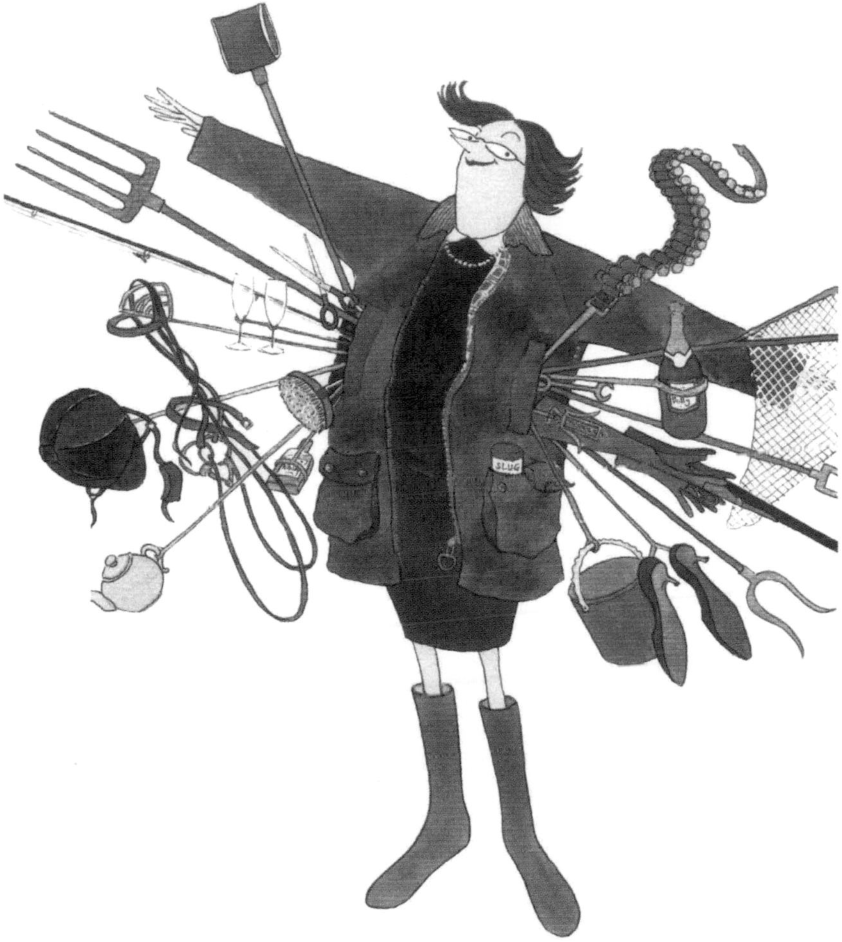
SLUG

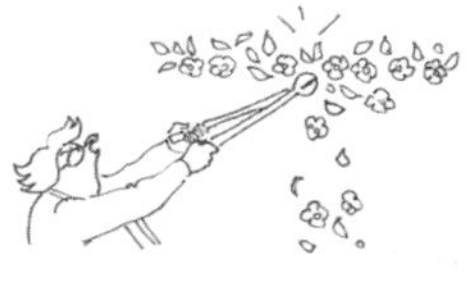

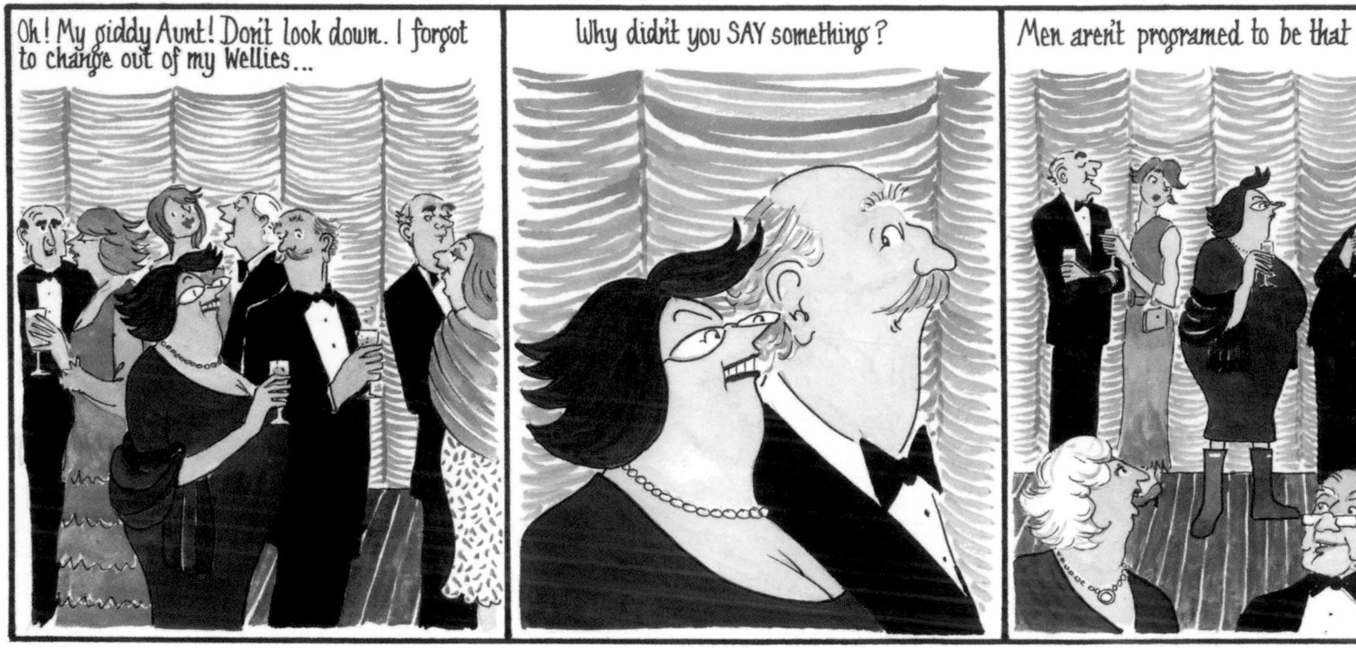
Oh! My giddy Aunt! Don't look down. I forgot to change out of my Wellies...
Why didn't you SAY something?
Men aren't programed to be that observant.

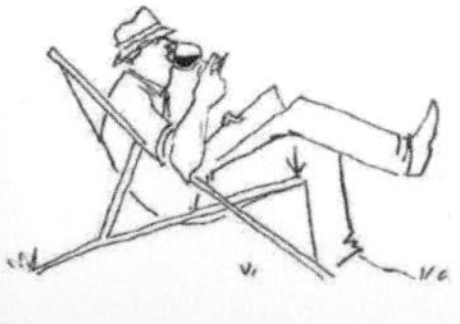

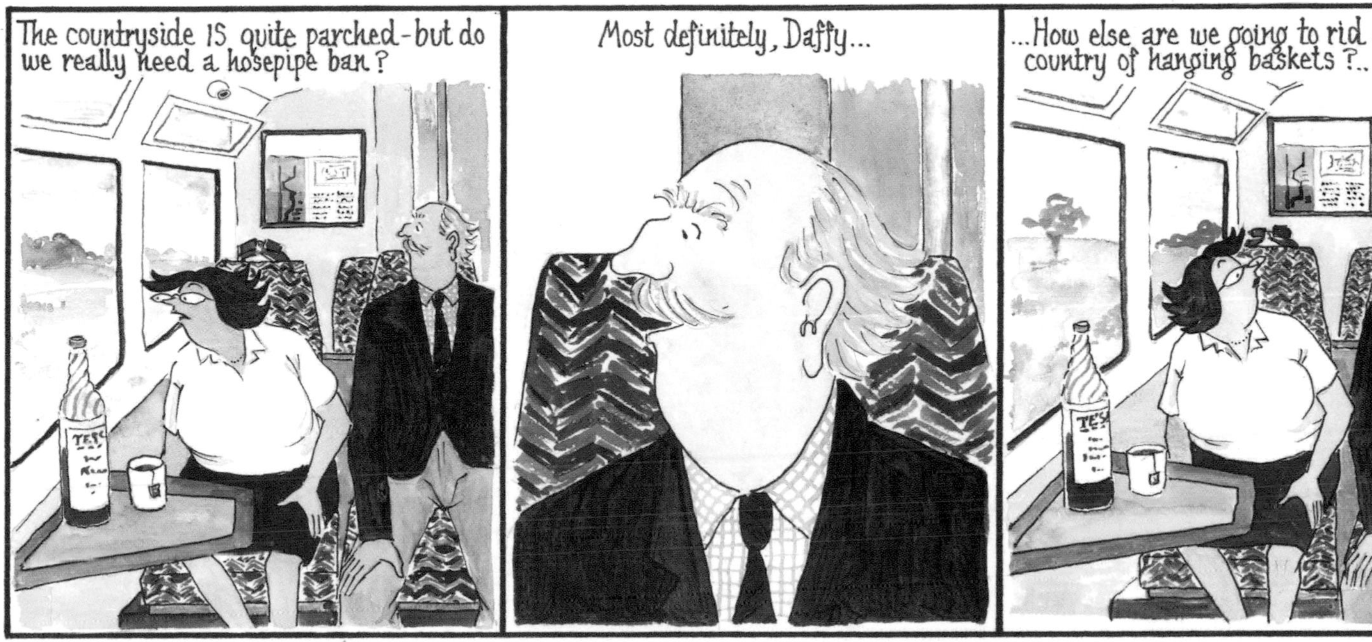
The countryside IS quite parched - but do we really need a hosepipe ban?
Most definitely, Daffy...
...How else are we going to rid our country of hanging baskets?..

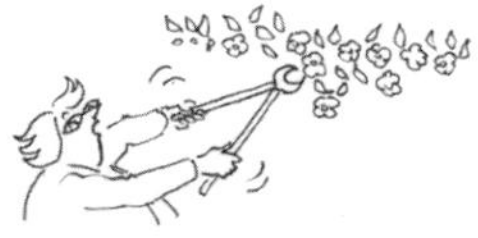

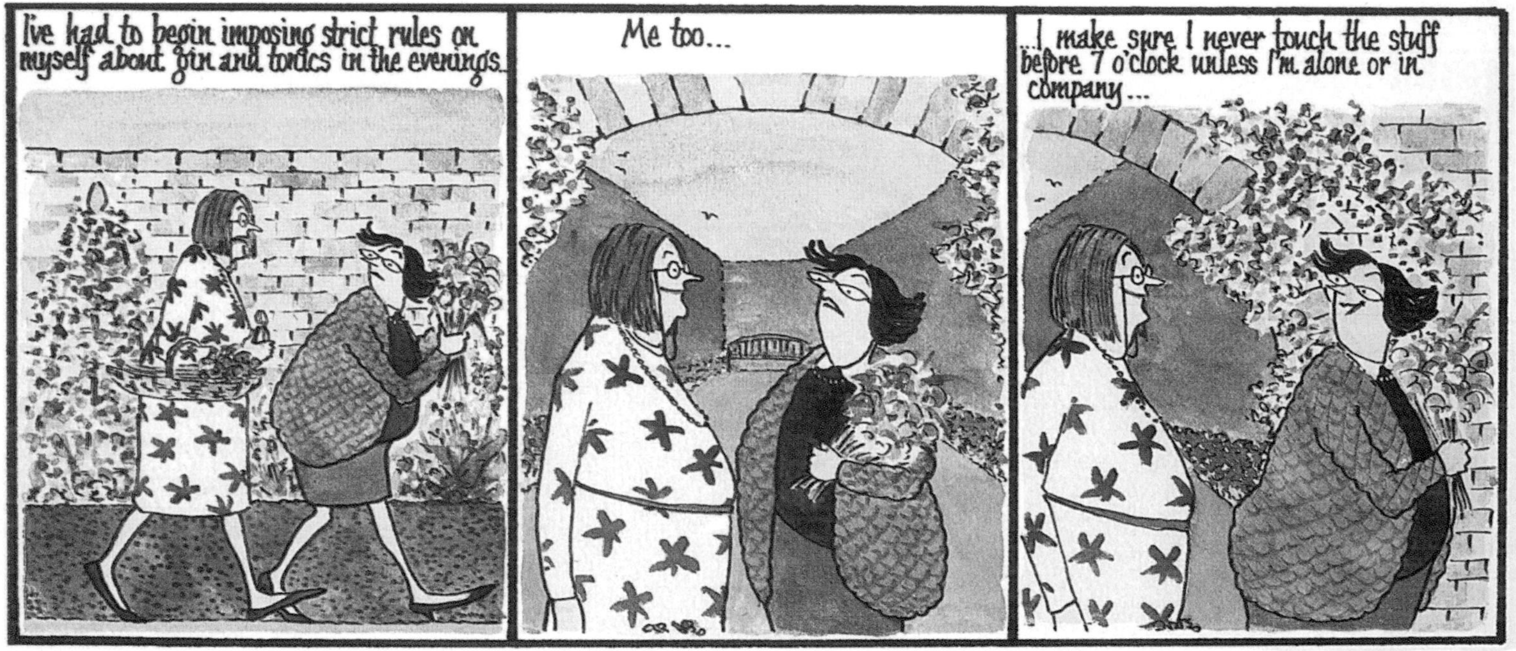
I've had to begin imposing strict rules on myself about gin and tonics in the evenings...
Me too...
...I make sure I never touch the stuff before 7 o'clock unless I'm alone or in company...

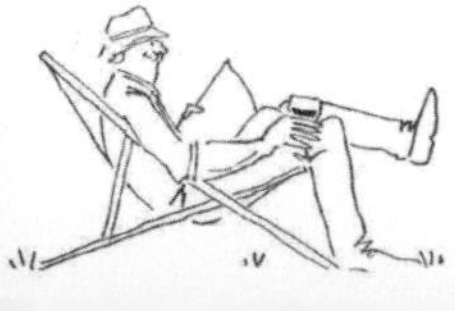

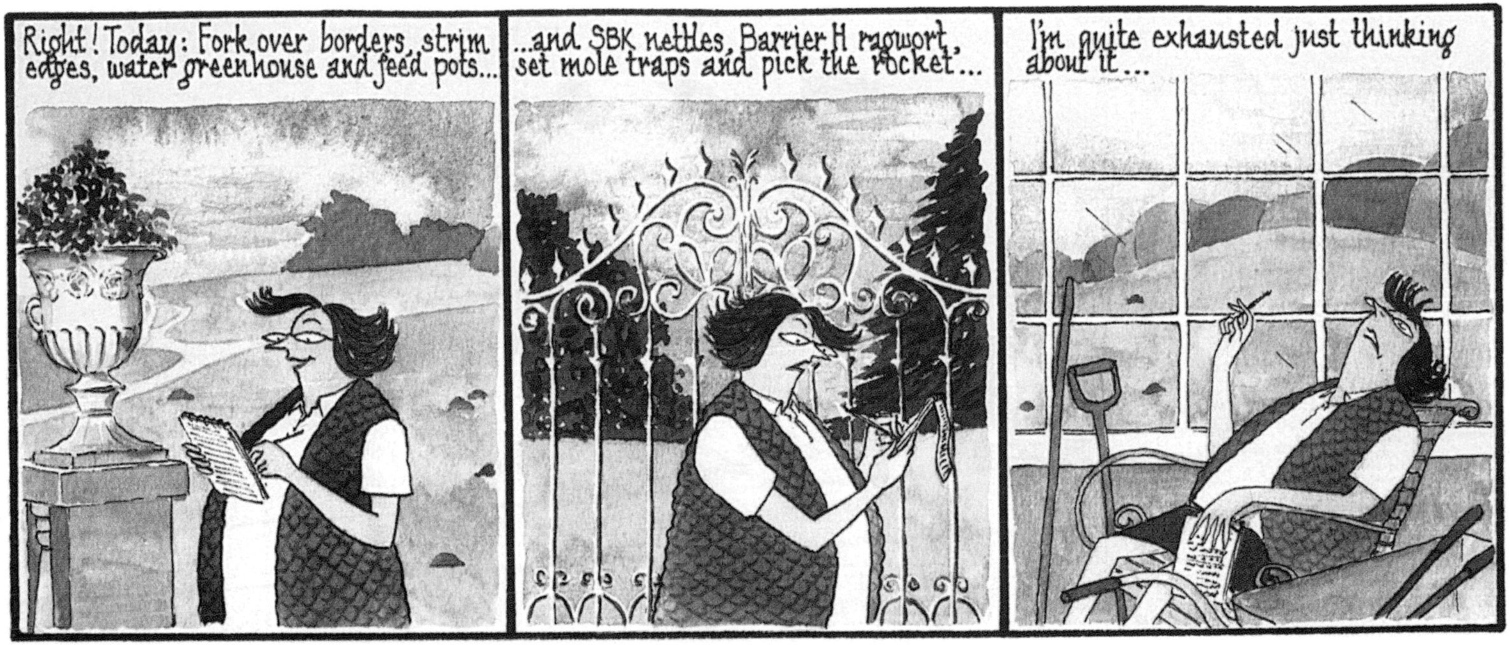
Right! Today: Fork over borders, strim edges, water greenhouse and feed pots...
...and SBK nettles, Barrier H ragwort, set mole traps and pick the rocket...
I'm quite exhausted just thinking about it...

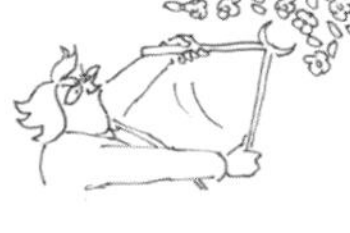

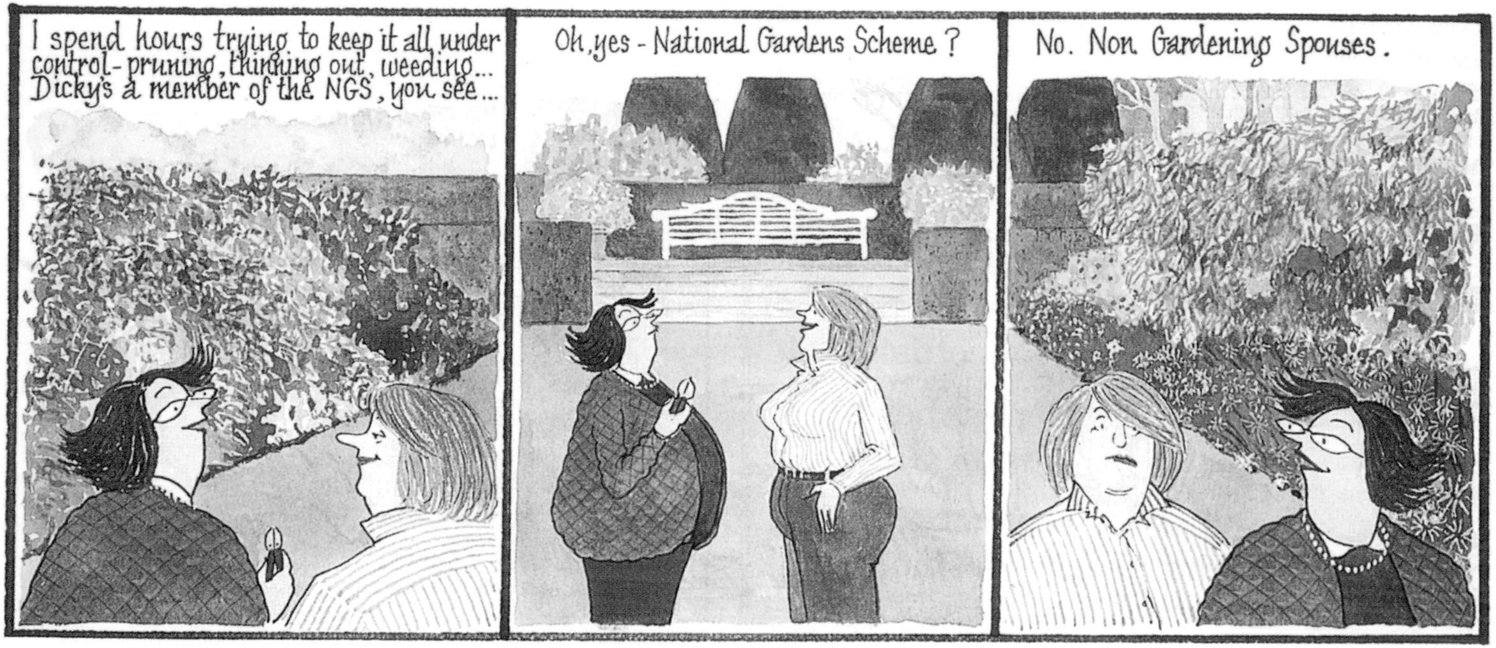
I spend hours trying to keep it all under control - pruning, thinning out, weeding... Dicky's a member of the NGS, you see...
Oh, yes - National Gardens Scheme?
No. Non Gardening Spouses.

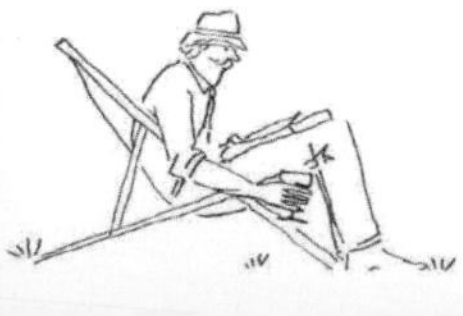

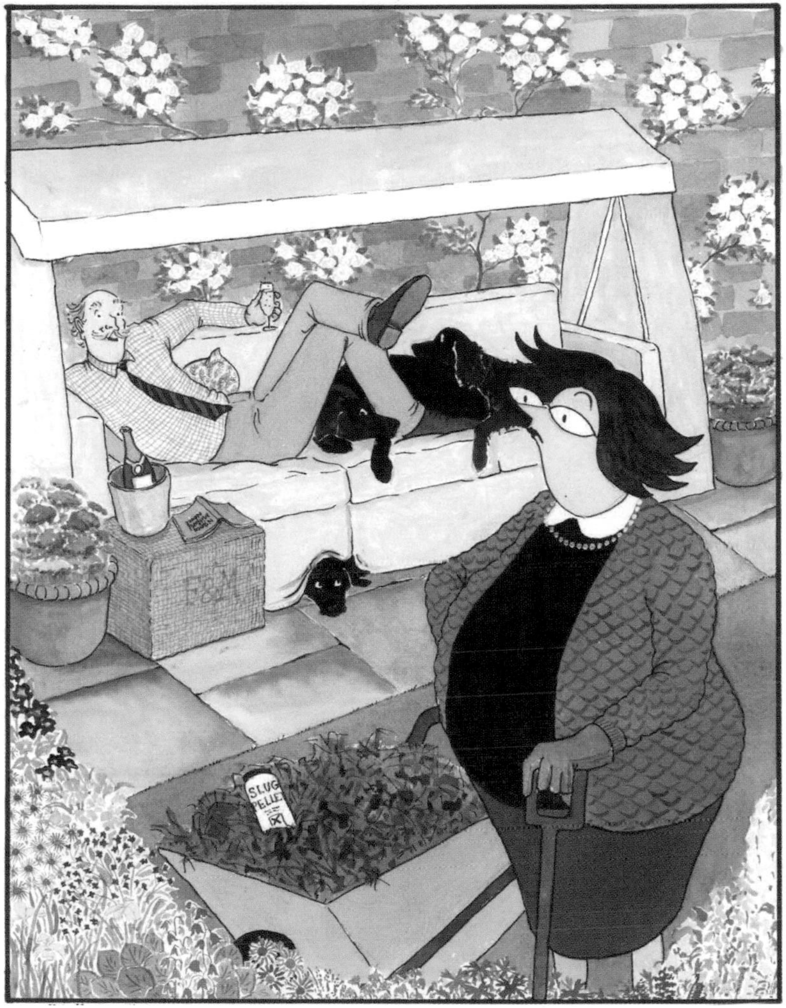
SLUG
PELLET

"What's the point of all your hard work in the garden if
I'm not allowed to sit down and enjoy it..."

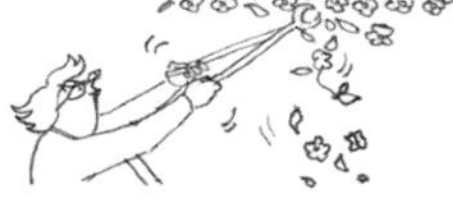

Never too old to ... play on the swings...

Never too old to ... climb trees...

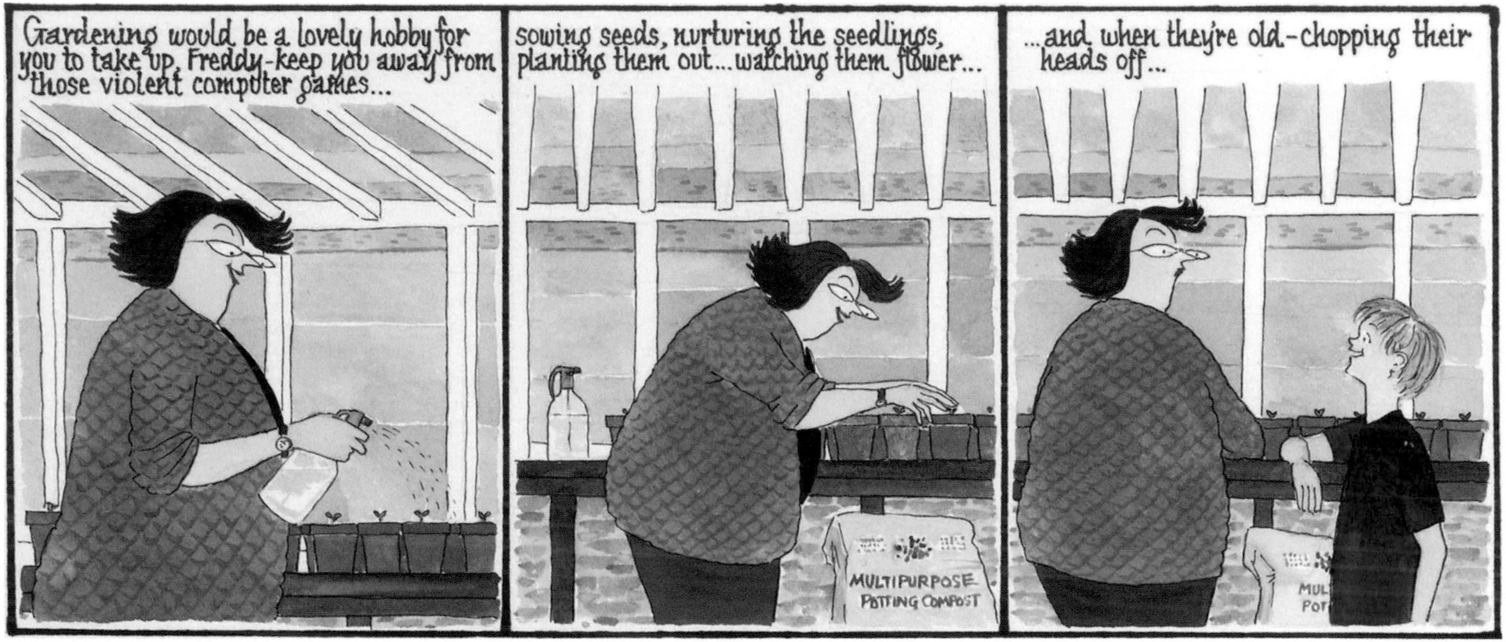
Gardening would be a lovely hobby for you to take up, Freddy-keep you away from those violent computer games...
sowing seeds, nurturing the seedlings, planting them out... watching them flower...
MULTIPURPOSE POTTING COMPOST
...and when they're old-chopping their heads off...

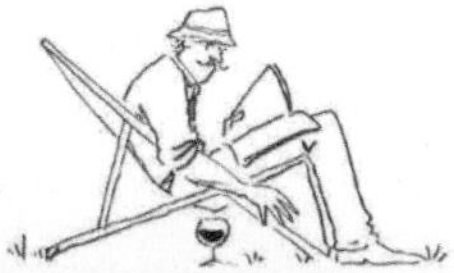

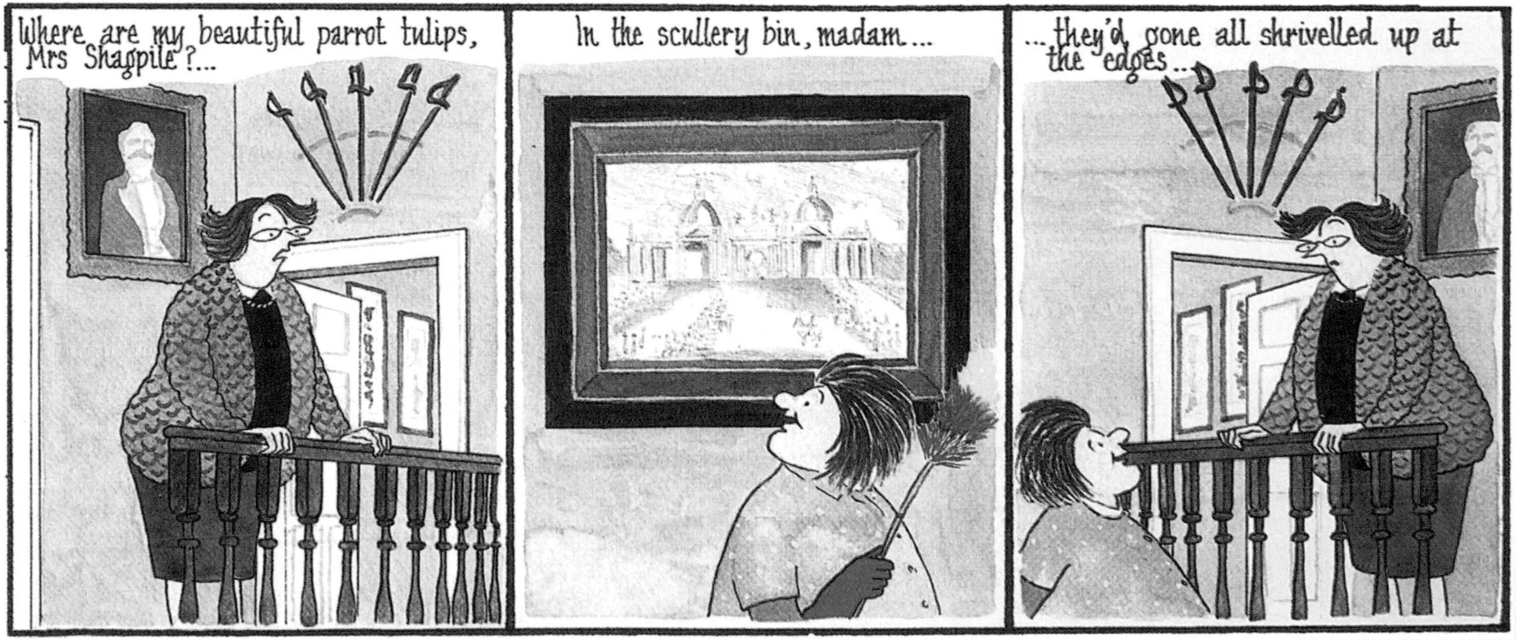
Where are my beautiful parrot tulips, Mrs Shagpile?...
In the scullery bin, madam...
...they'd gone all shrivelled up at the edges...

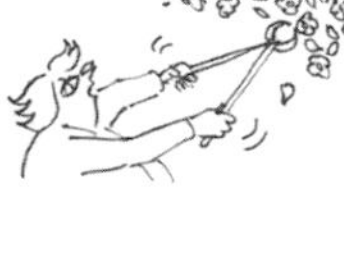

THERAPEUTIC WINTER JOBS: Pressure washing everything

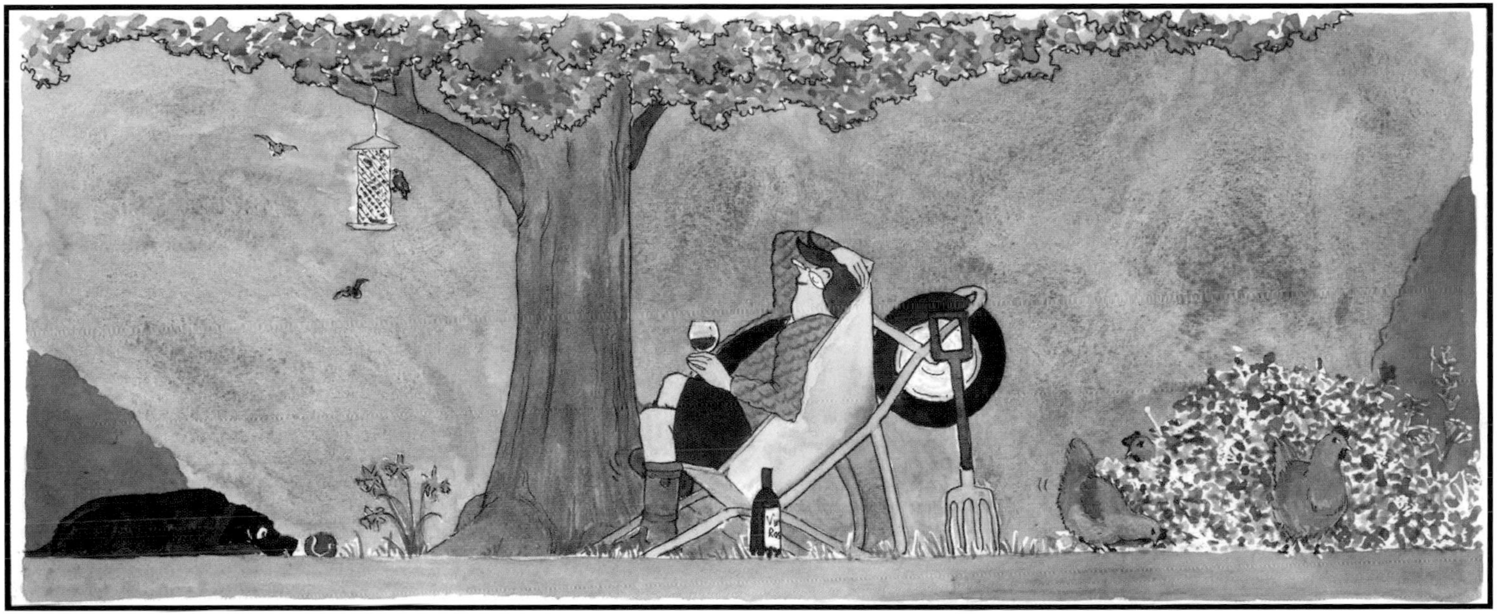

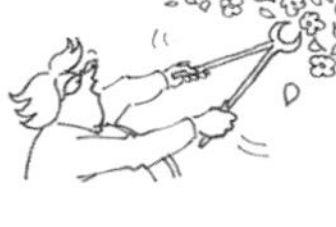

"There's another mole hill on my lawn...."

FEMALE SOLUTIONS: Molehills on the lawn

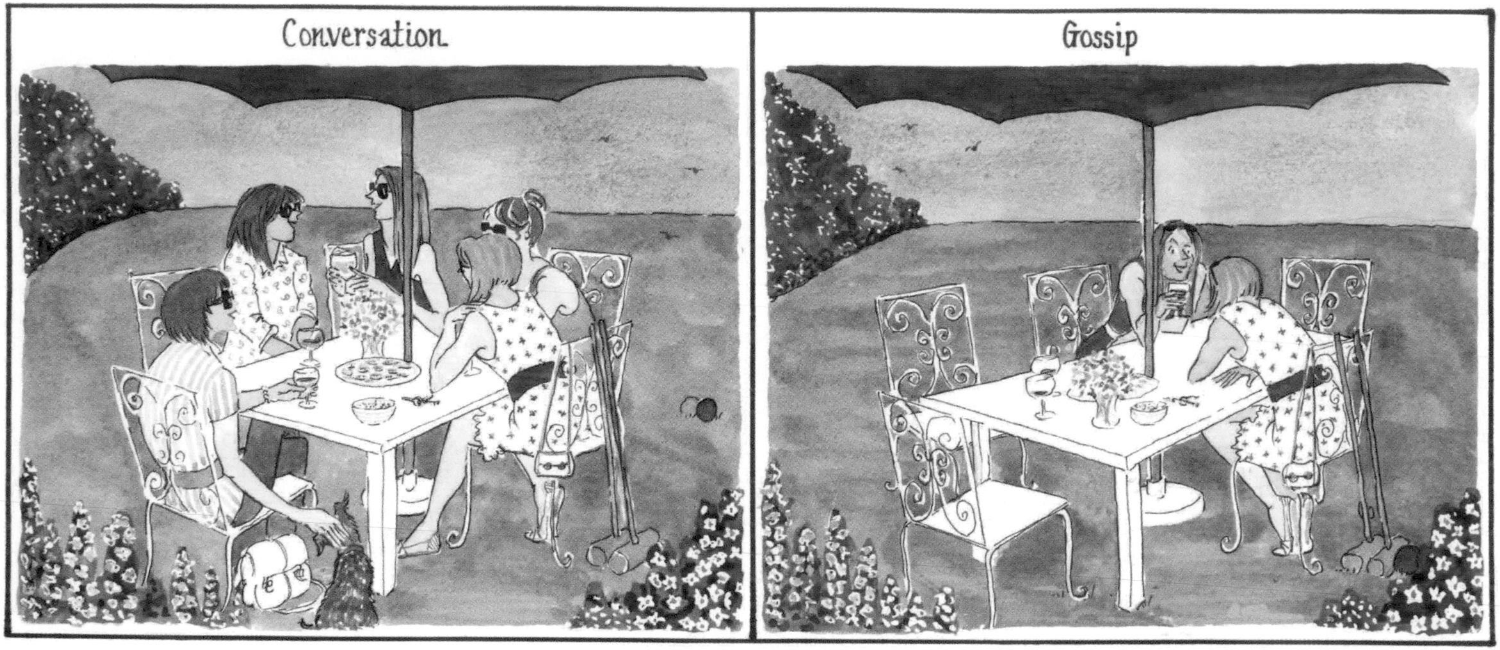
Conversation
Gossip

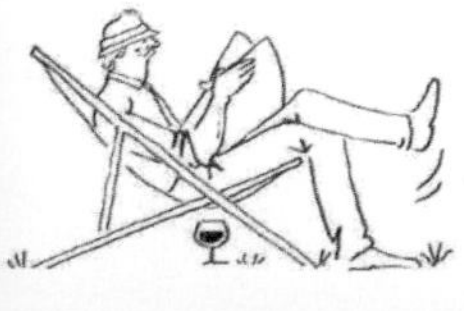

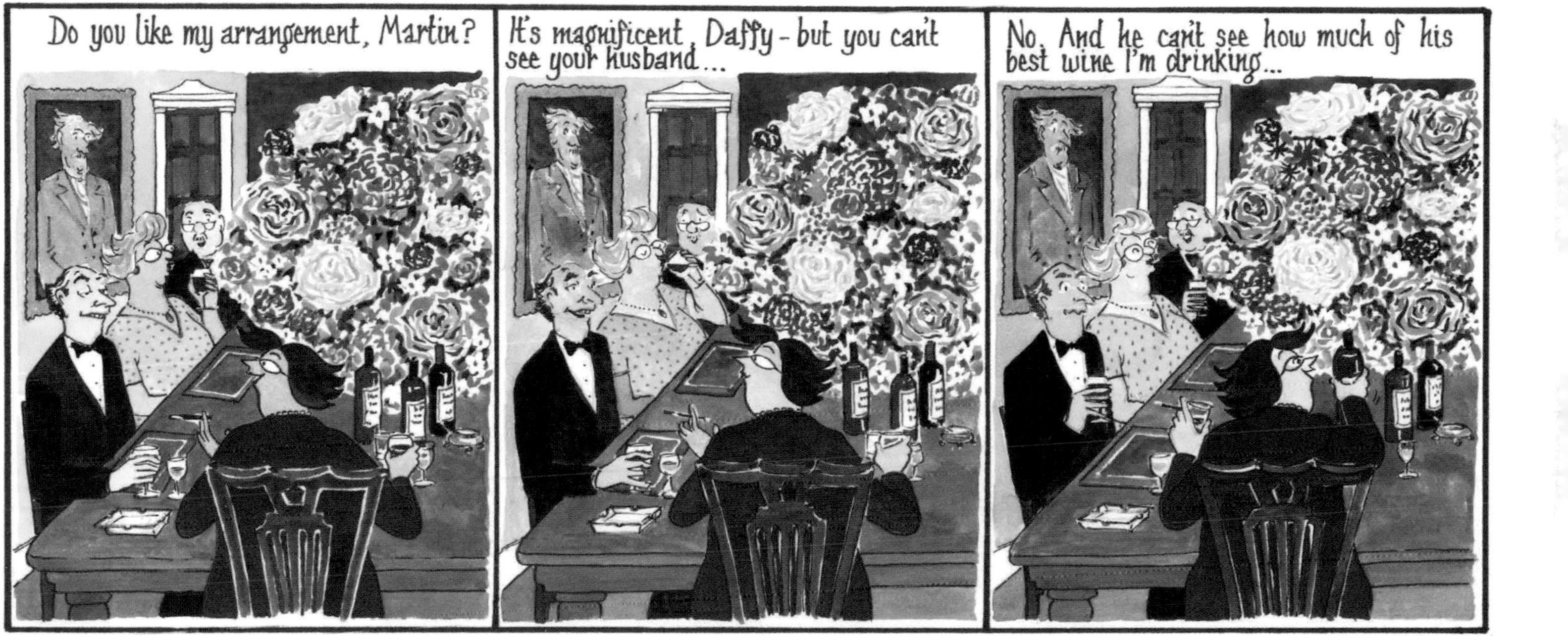
Do you like my arrangement, Martin?
It's magnificent, Daffy - but you can't see your husband...
No. And he can't see how much of his best wine I'm drinking...

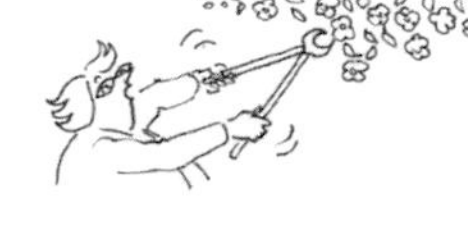

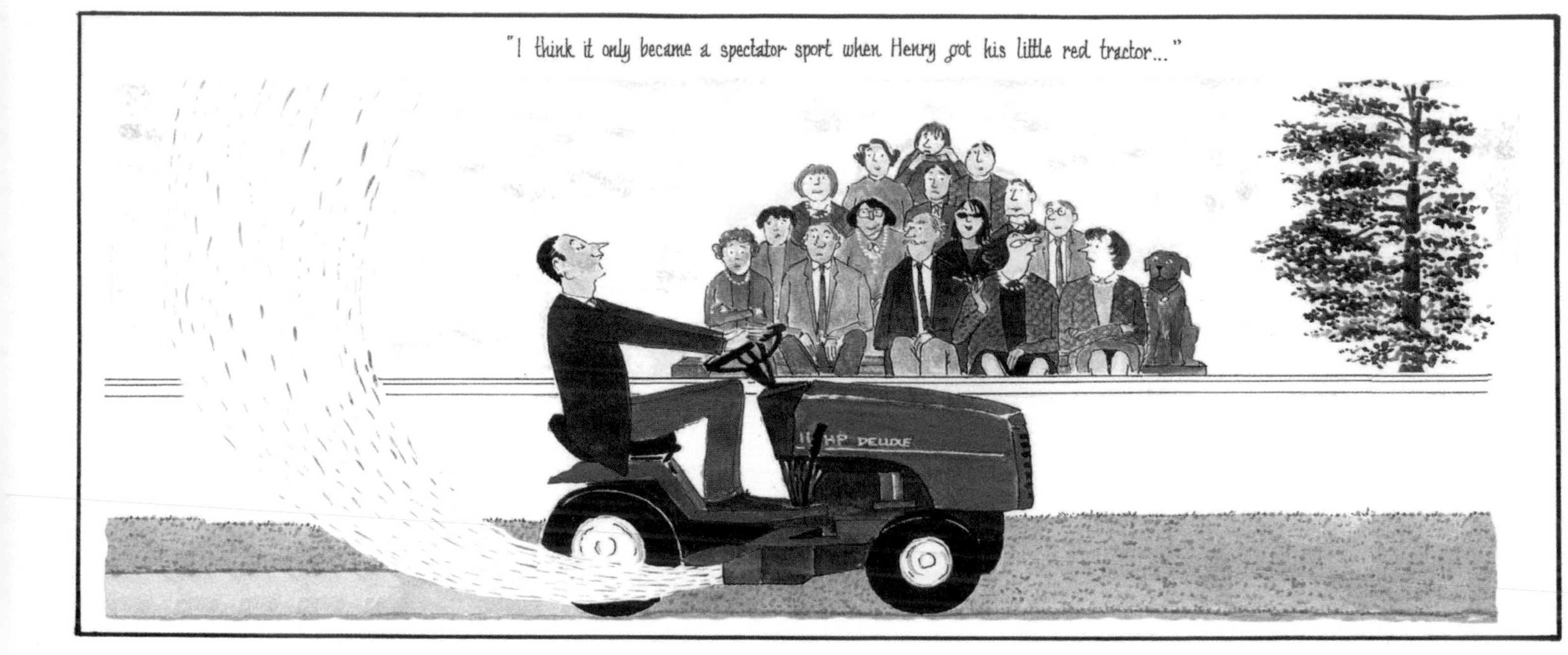
HP DELUXE

"I think it only became a spectator sport when Henry got his little red tractor..."

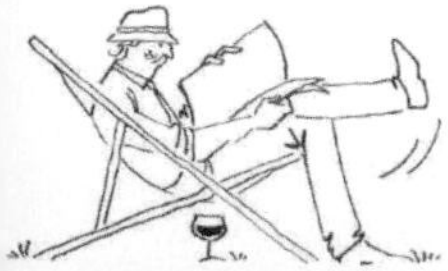

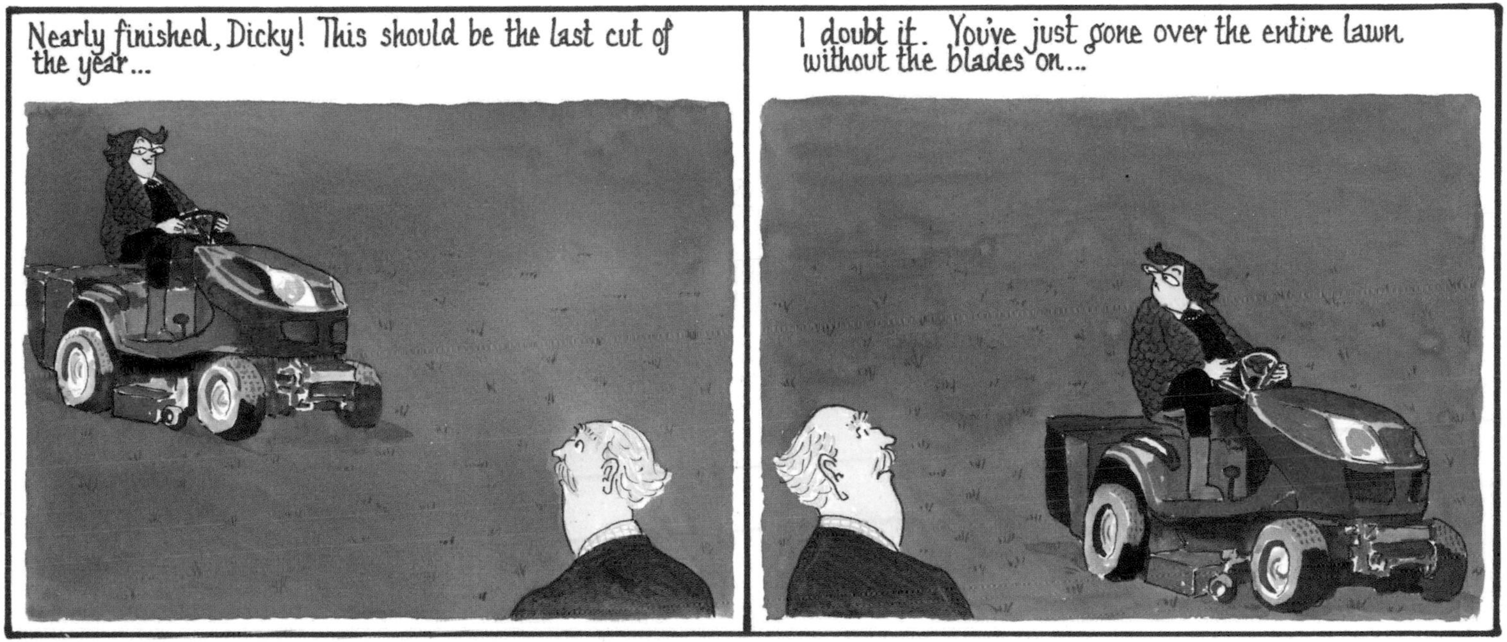
Nearly finished, Dicky! This should be the last cut of the year...
I doubt it. You've just gone over the entire lawn without the blades on...

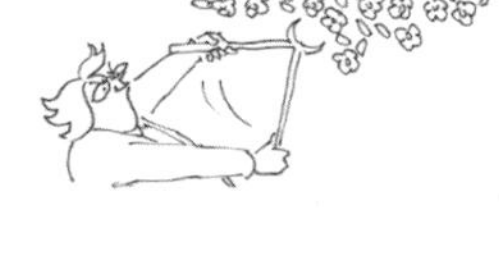

You know you're getting older when...
Lawn care becomes the highlight of your life!

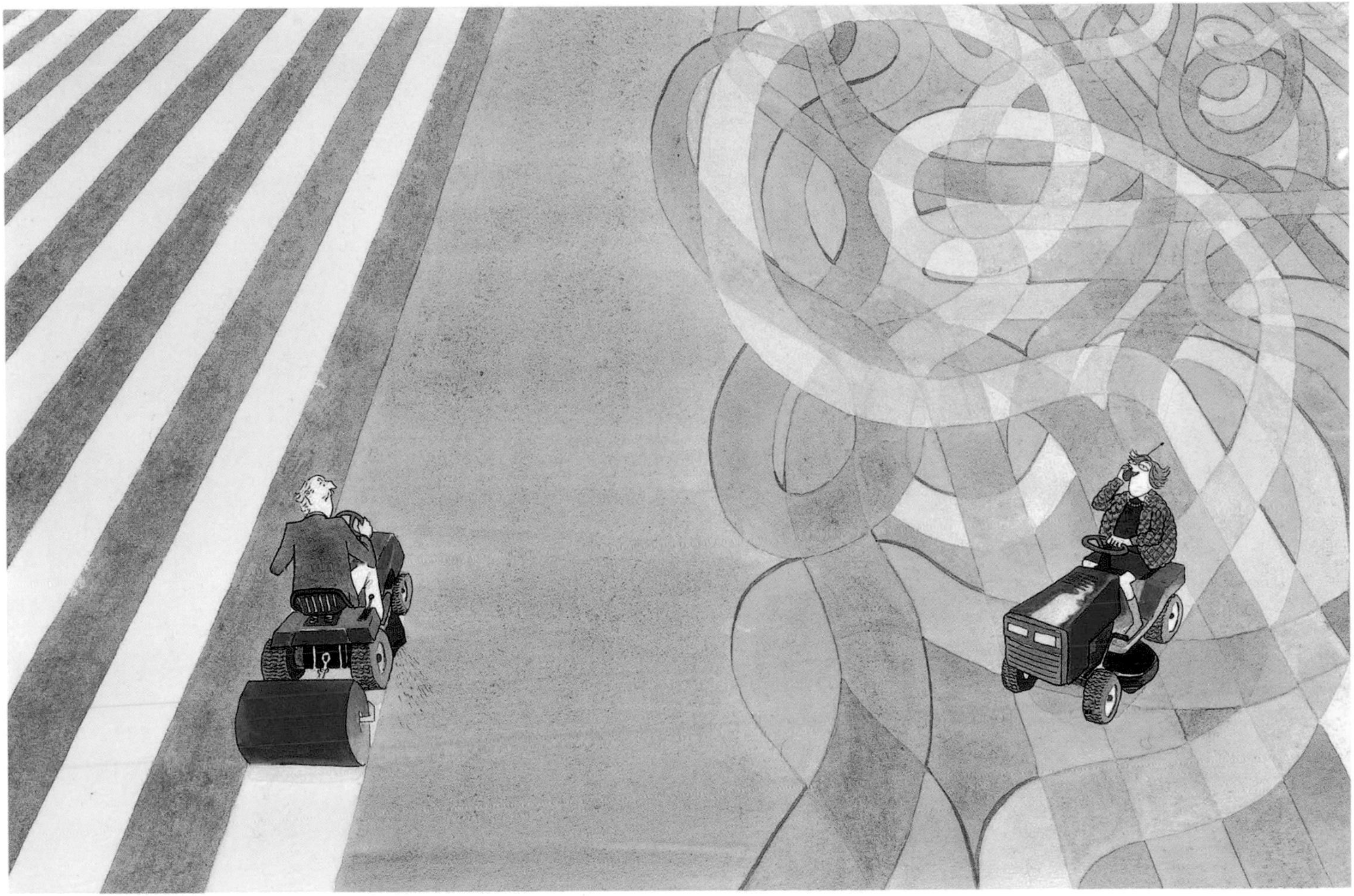

Mars and Venus mow the lawn...

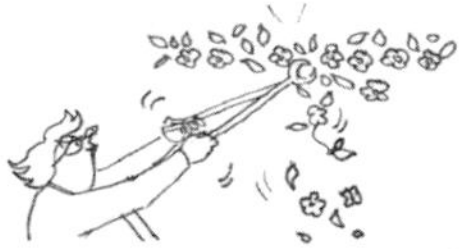

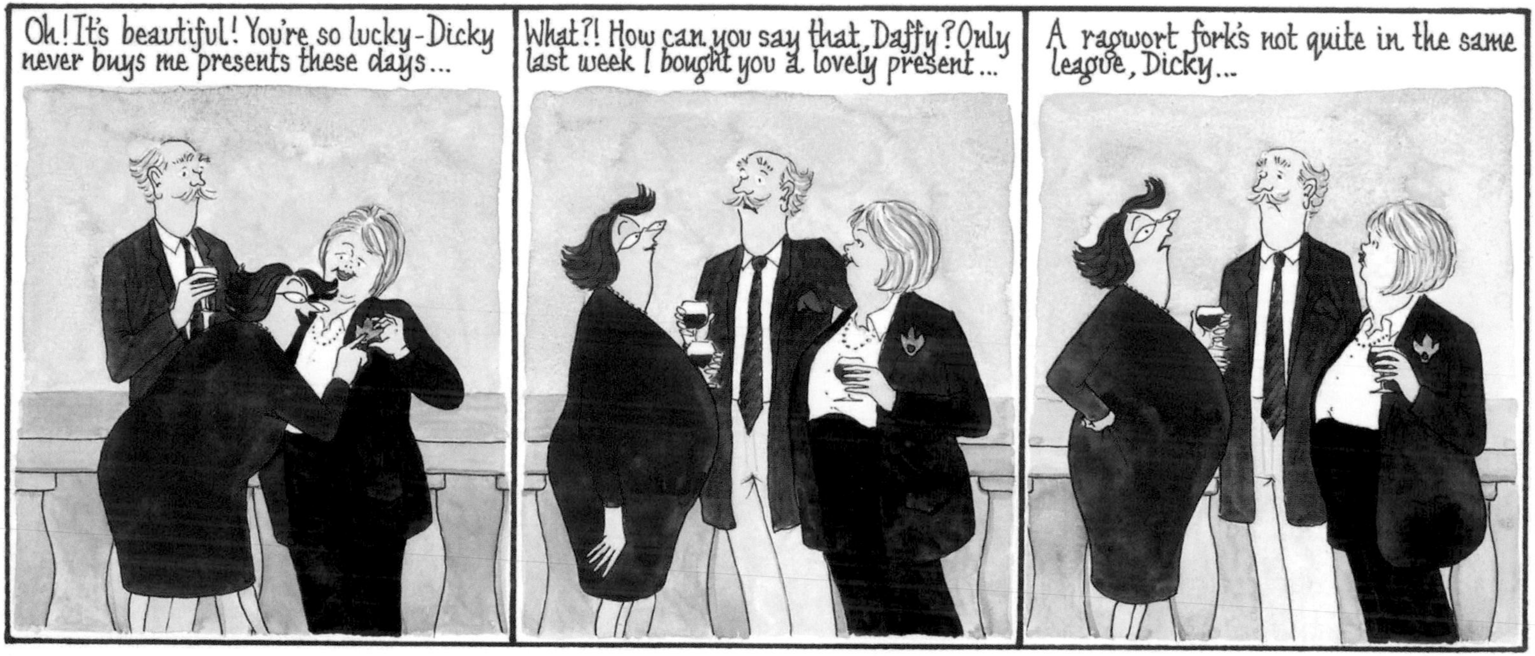
Oh! It's beautiful! You're so lucky - Dicky never buys me presents these days...
What?! How can you say that, Daffy? Only last week I bought you a lovely present...
A ragwort fork's not quite in the same league, Dicky...

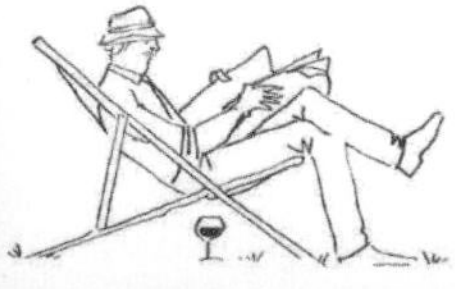

GREAT GARDENING MOMENTS ... KNOWING THE LATIN NAME

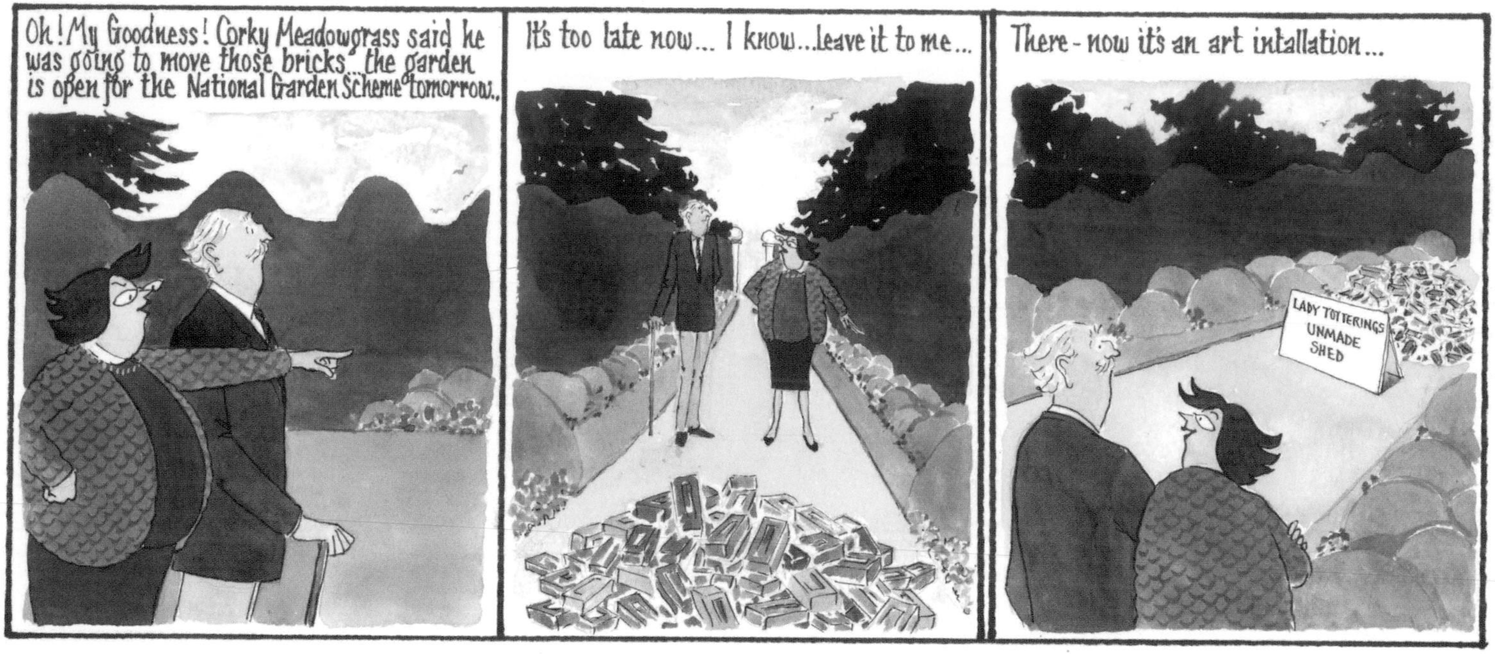
Oh! My Goodness! Corky Meadowgrass said he was going to move those bricks... the garden is open for the National Garden Scheme tomorrow..
It's too late now... I know... leave it to me...
There - now it's an art intallation...
LADY TOTTERINGS UNMADE SHED

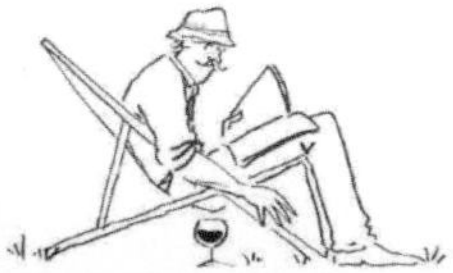

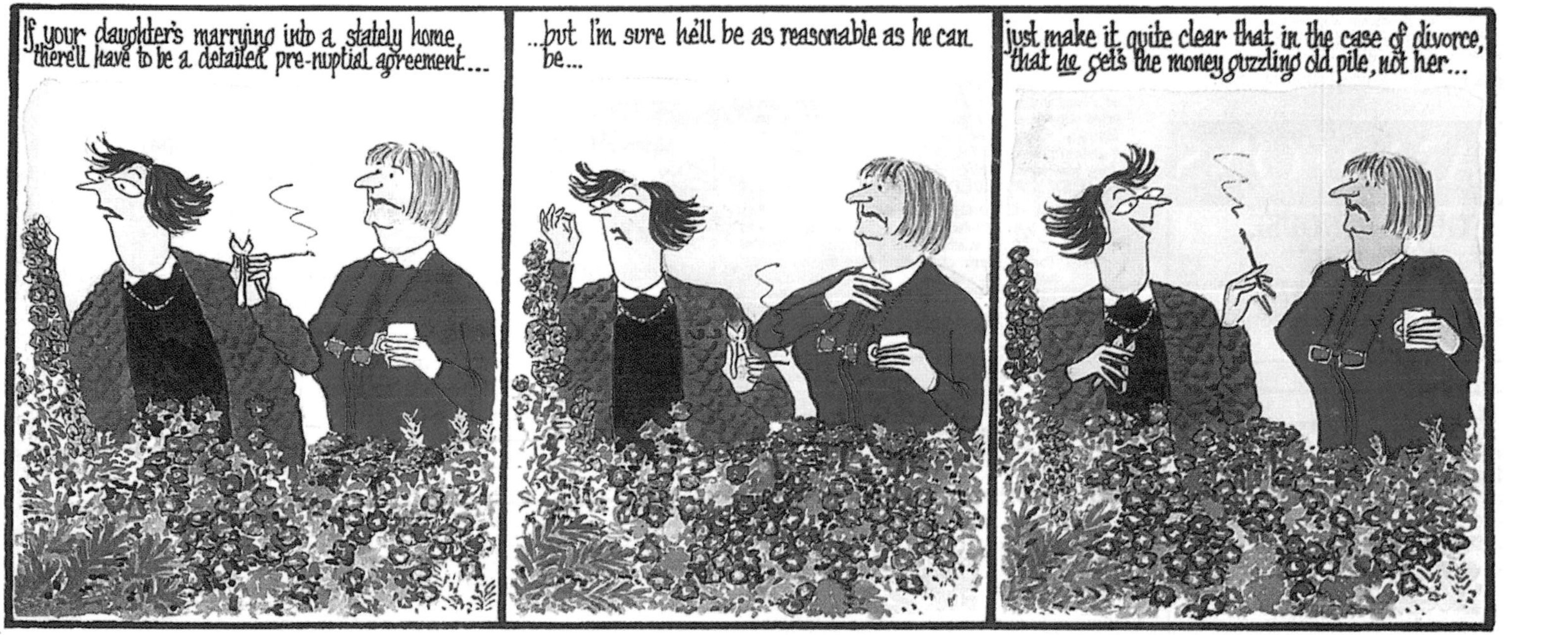
If your daughter's marrying into a stately home, there'll have to be a detailed pre-nuptial agreement...
...but I'm sure he'll be as reasonable as he can be...
just make it quite clear that in the case of divorce, that he gets the money guzzling old pile, not her...

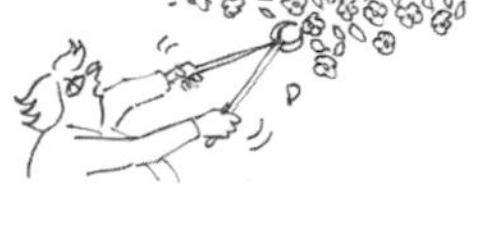

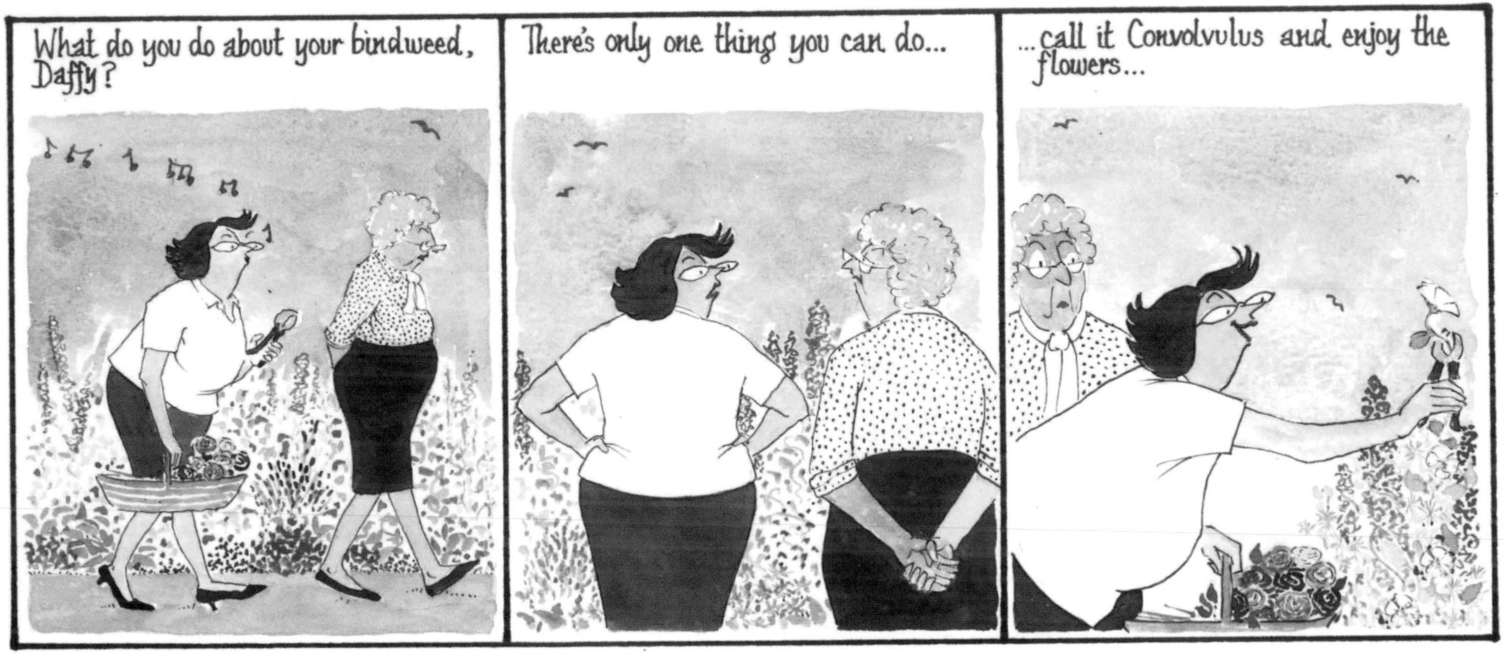
What do you do about your bindweed, Daffy?
There's only one thing you can do...
...call it Convolvulus and enjoy the flowers...

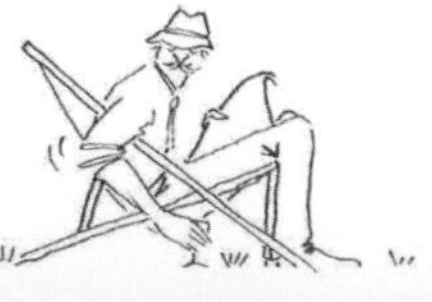

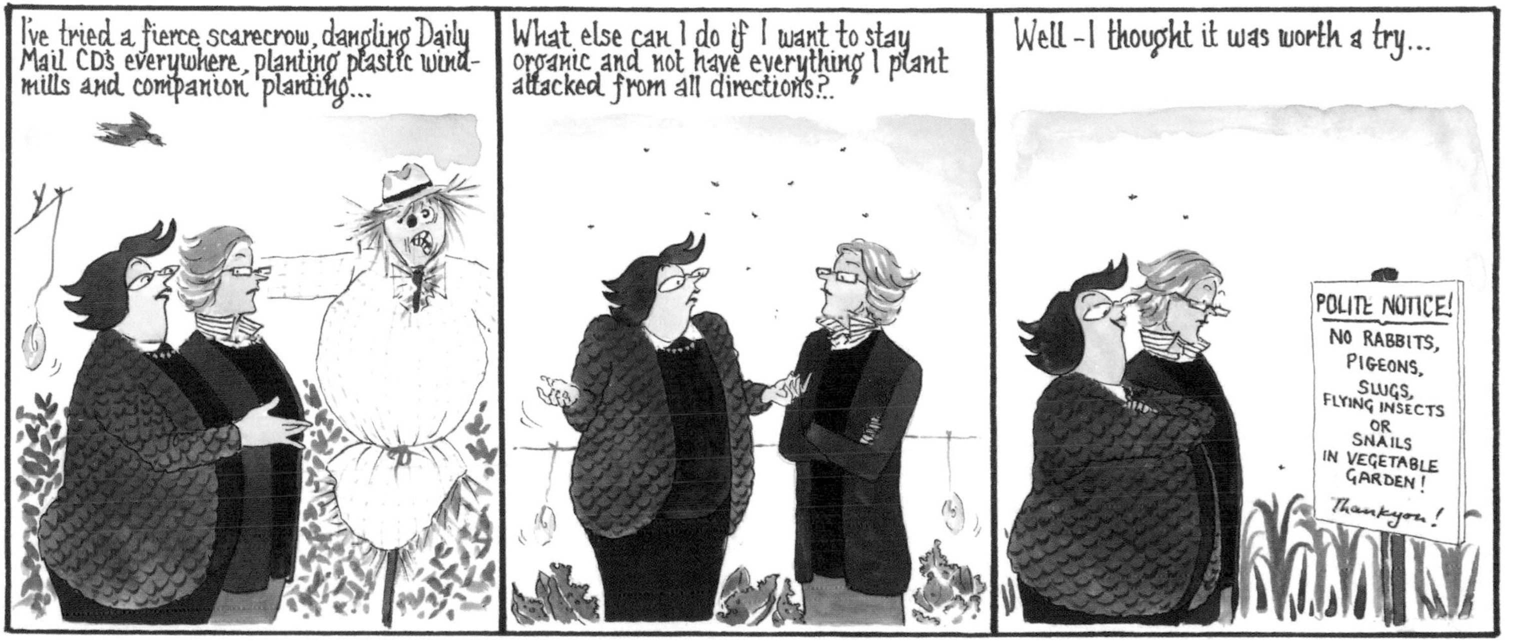
I've tried a fierce scarecrow, dangling Daily Mail CD's everywhere, planting plastic windmills and companion planting...
What else can I do if I want to stay organic and not have everything I plant attacked from all directions?..
Well - I thought it was worth a try...
POLITE NOTICE!
NO RABBITS, PIGEONS, SLUGS, FLYING INSECTS OR SNAILS IN VEGETABLE GARDEN!
Thankyou!

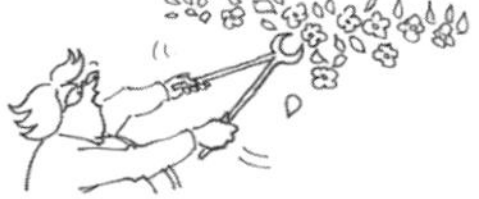

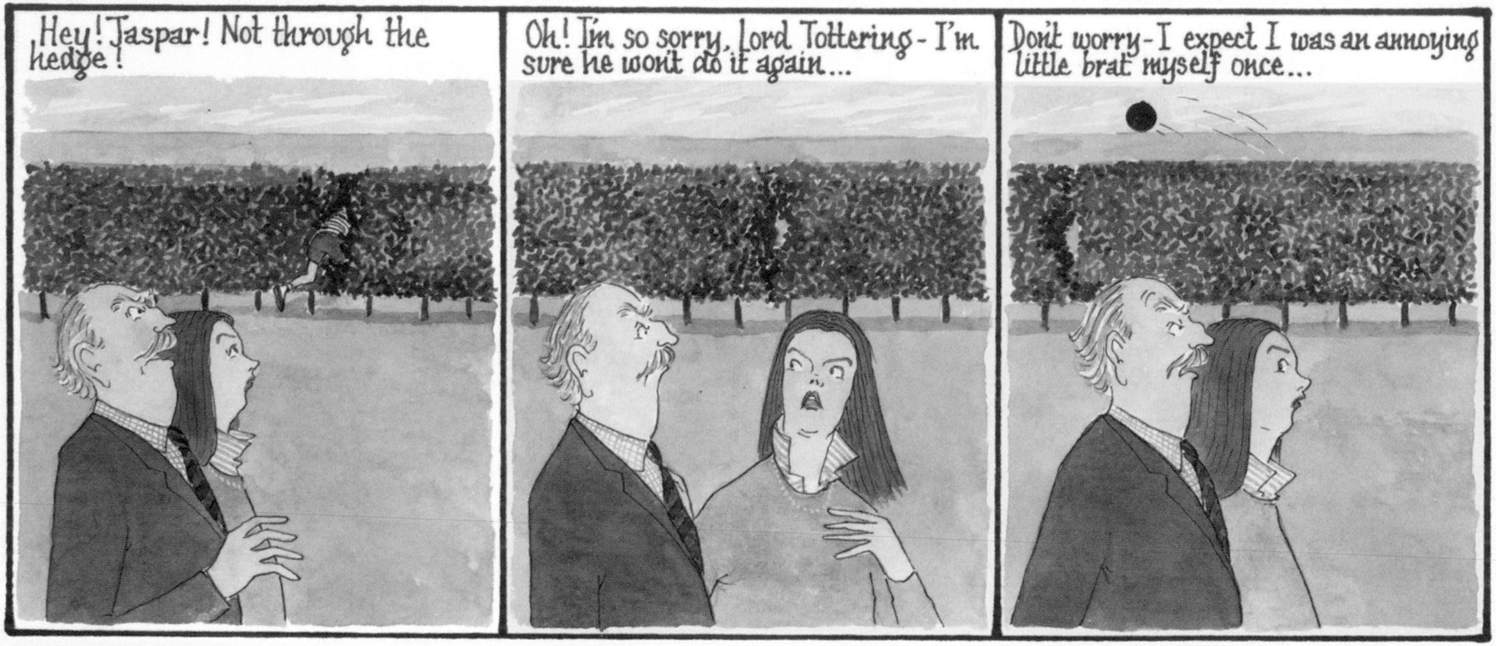
Hey! Jaspar! Not through the hedge!
Oh! I'm so sorry, Lord Tottering - I'm sure he won't do it again...
Don't worry - I expect I was an annoying little brat myself once...

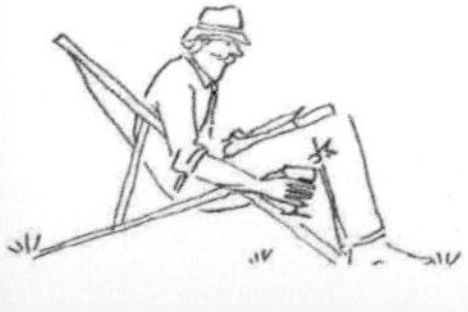

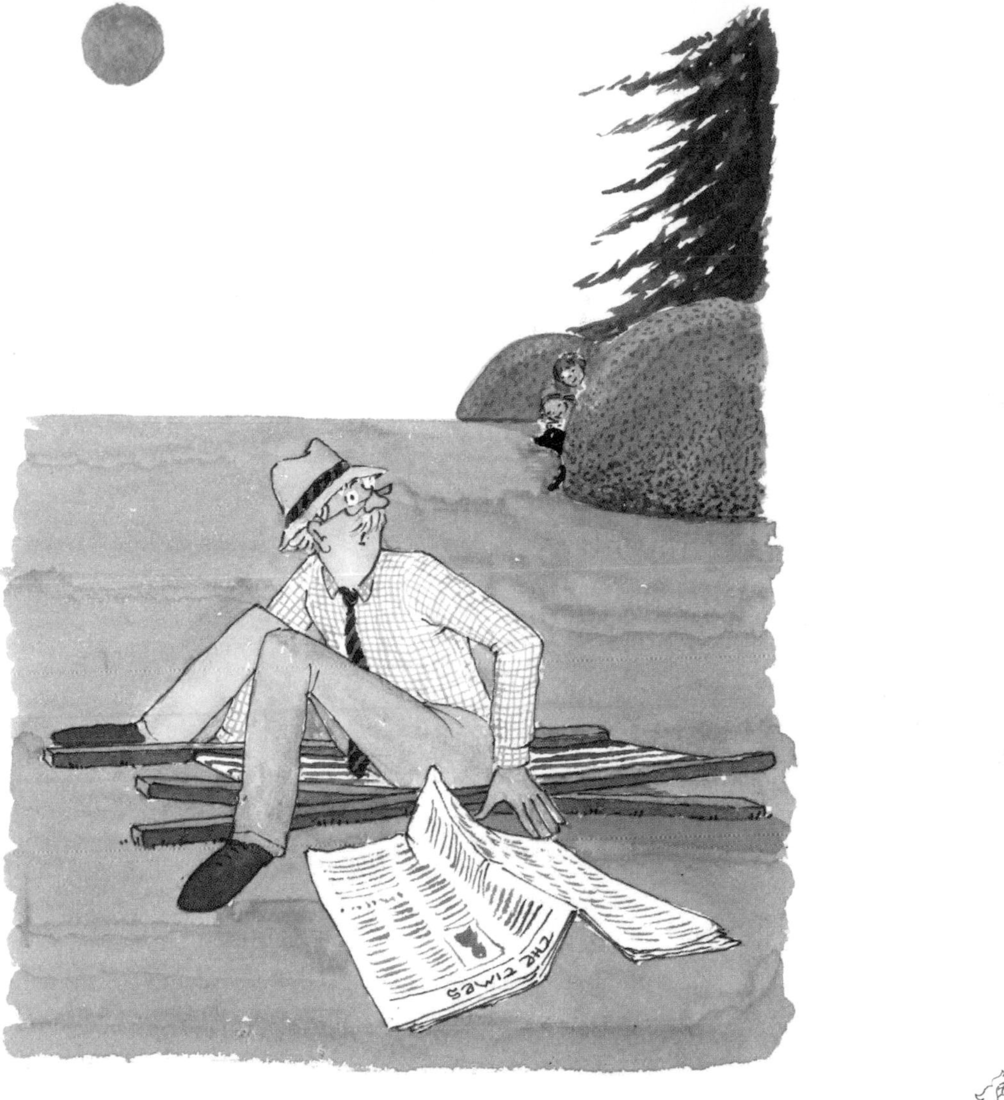
THE TIMES

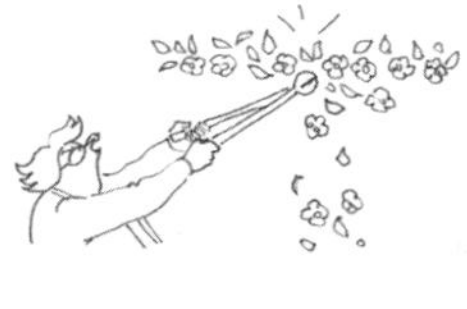

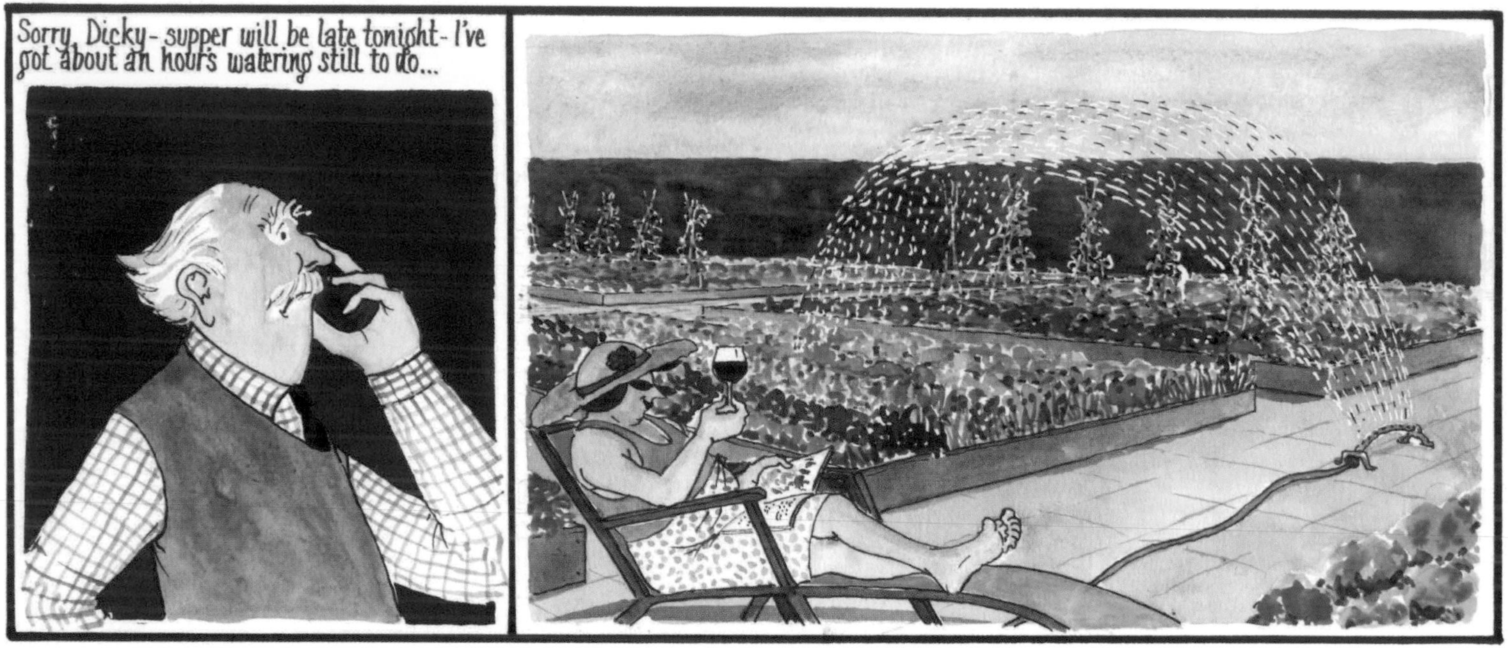
Sorry, Dicky - supper will be late tonight - I've got about an hour's watering still to do...

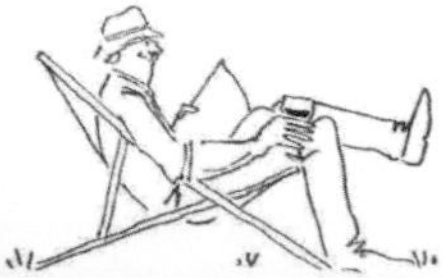

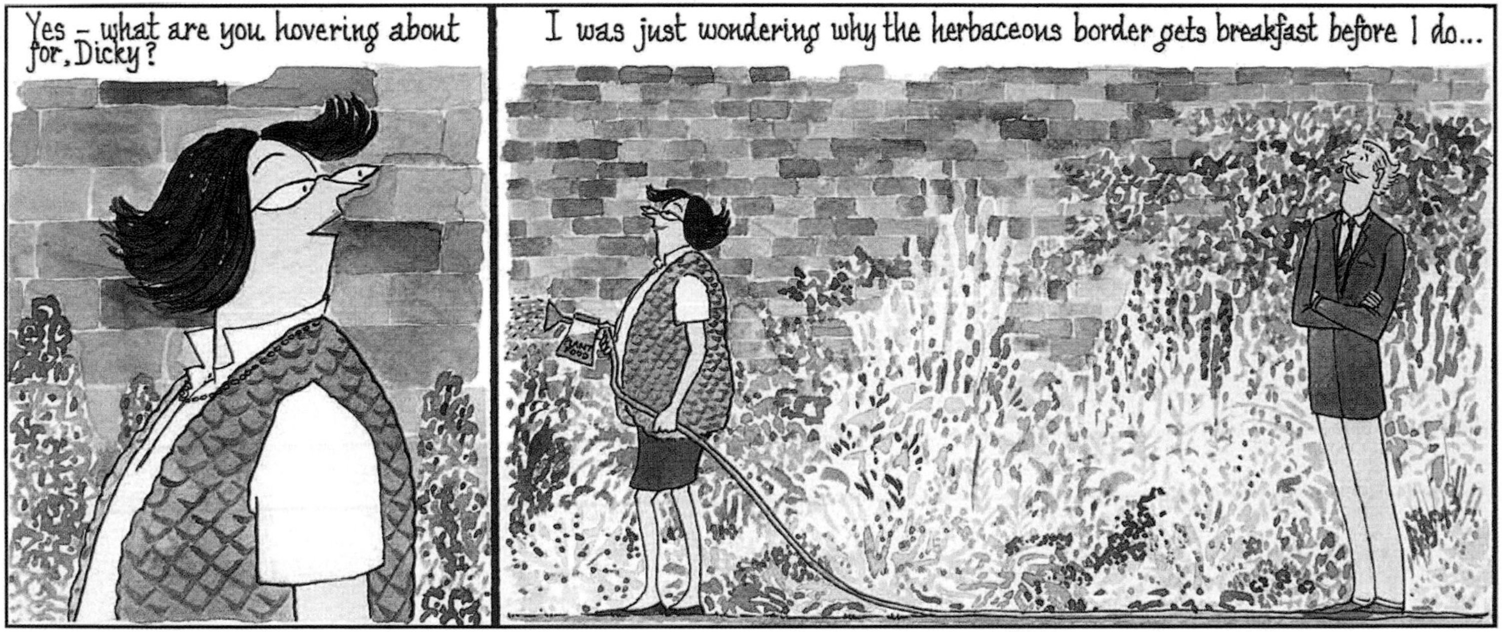
Yes – what are you hovering about for, Dicky?
I was just wondering why the herbaceous border gets breakfast before I do...

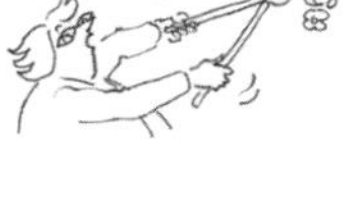

"If they used to have 25 indoor staff at Audley End, I hardly think the family did all the weeding themselves like you do..."

"Osborne House was built by Queen Victoria
and Prince Albert, but I live here now ..."

THE FEMALE CHARACTER: A tendency to succumb to a loud 'horizontal life pause' after a second glass of Rosé in the garden...

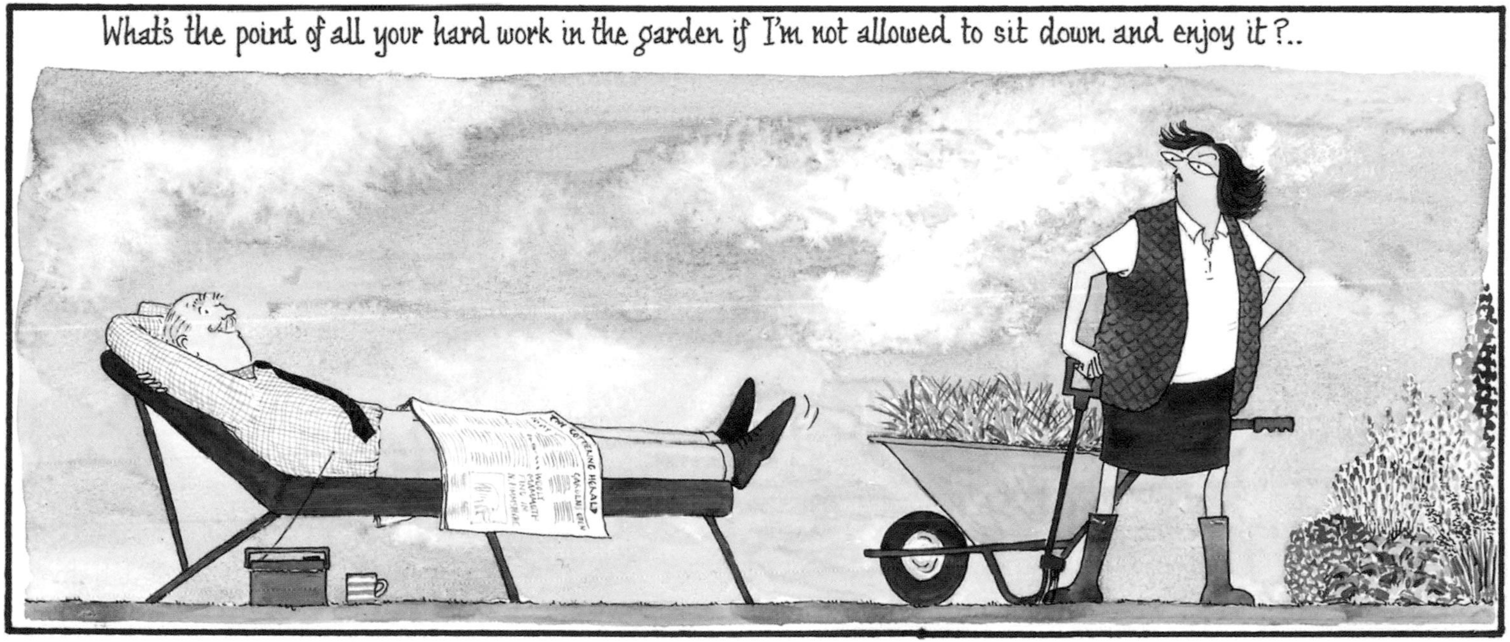

What's the point of all your hard work in the garden if I'm not allowed to sit down and enjoy it?..

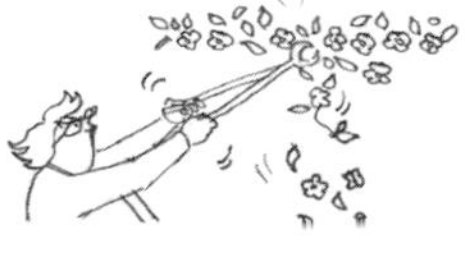

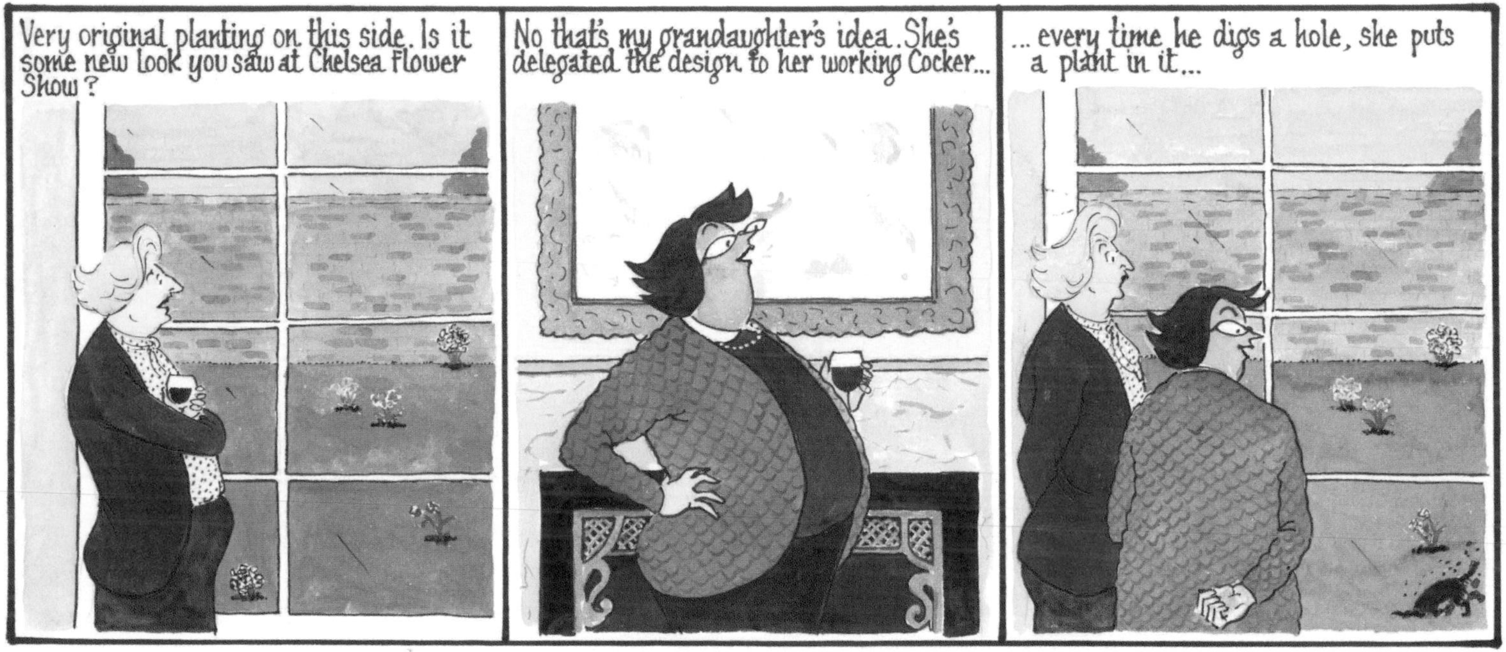
Very original planting on this side. Is it some new look you saw at Chelsea Flower Show?
No that's my grandaughter's idea. She's delegated the design to her working Cocker...
... every time he digs a hole, she puts a plant in it...

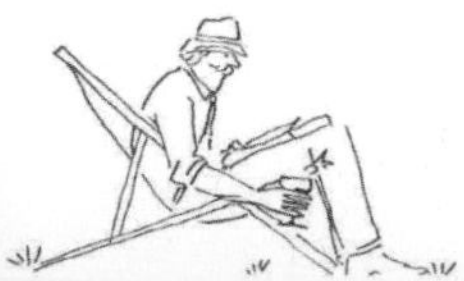

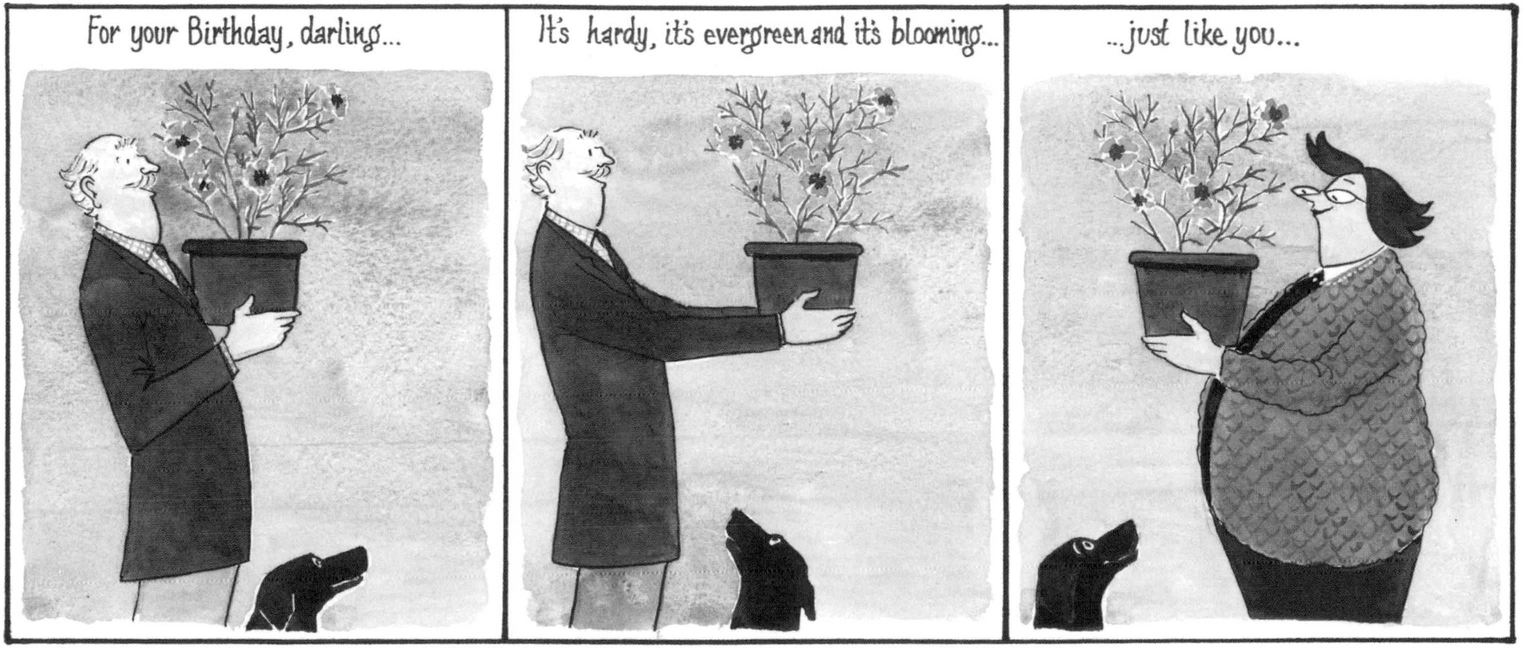
For your Birthday, darling...
It's hardy, it's evergreen and it's blooming...
...just like you...

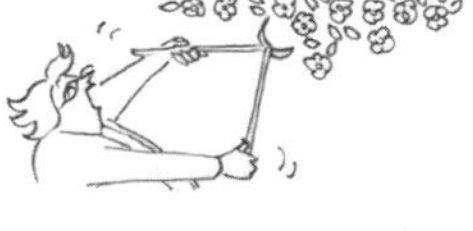

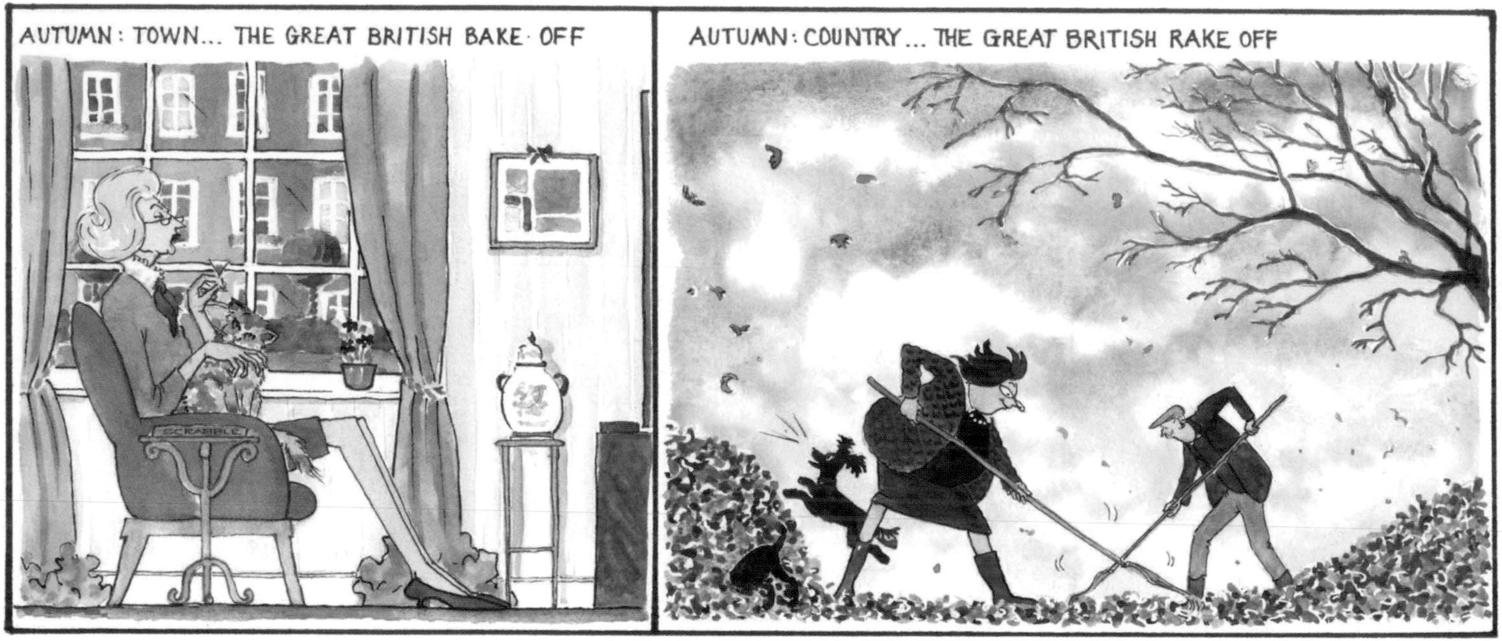
AUTUMN: TOWN... THE GREAT BRITISH BAKE·OFF
SCRABBLE
AUTUMN: COUNTRY... THE GREAT BRITISH RAKE OFF

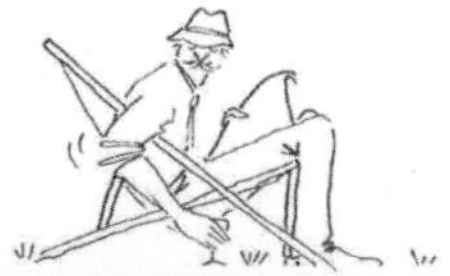

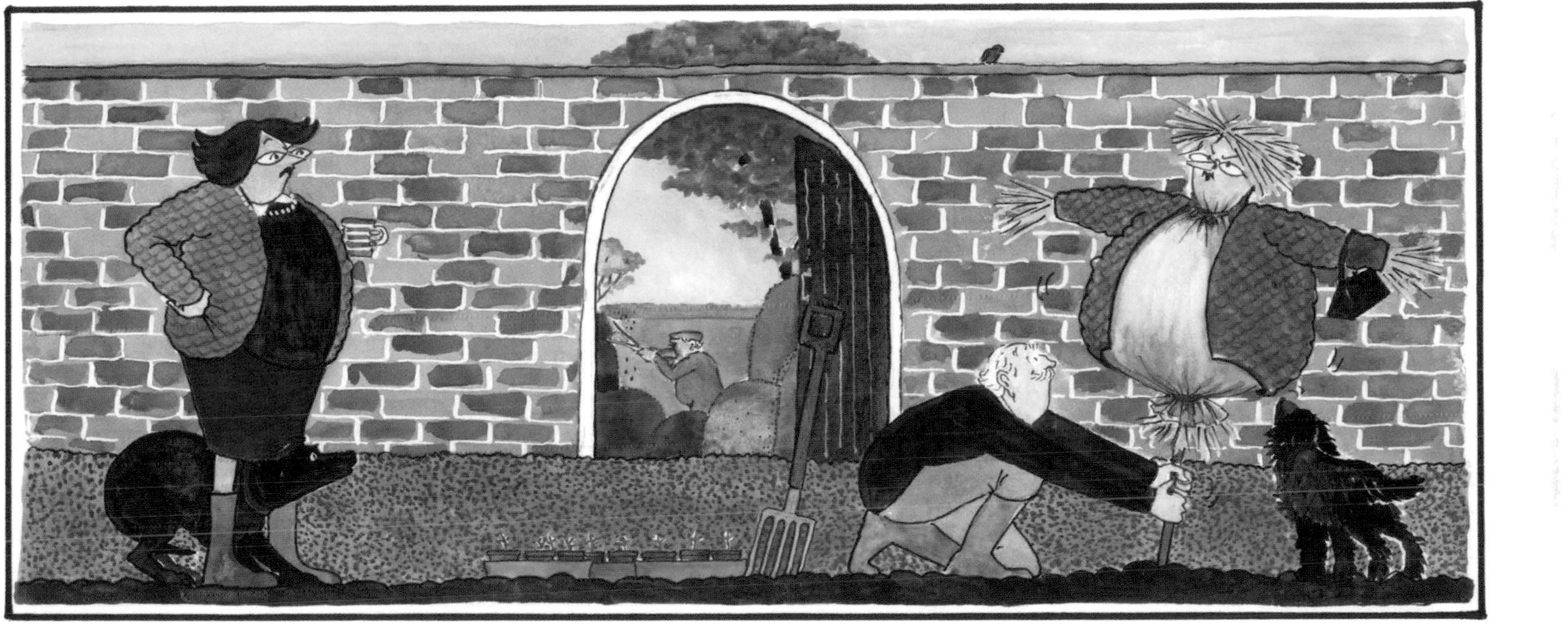

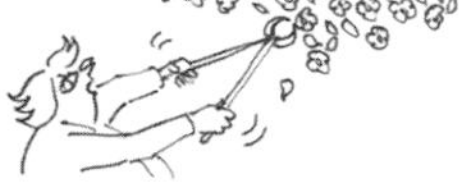

This way we won't get annoyed when we can't remember simple names like Delphiniums...

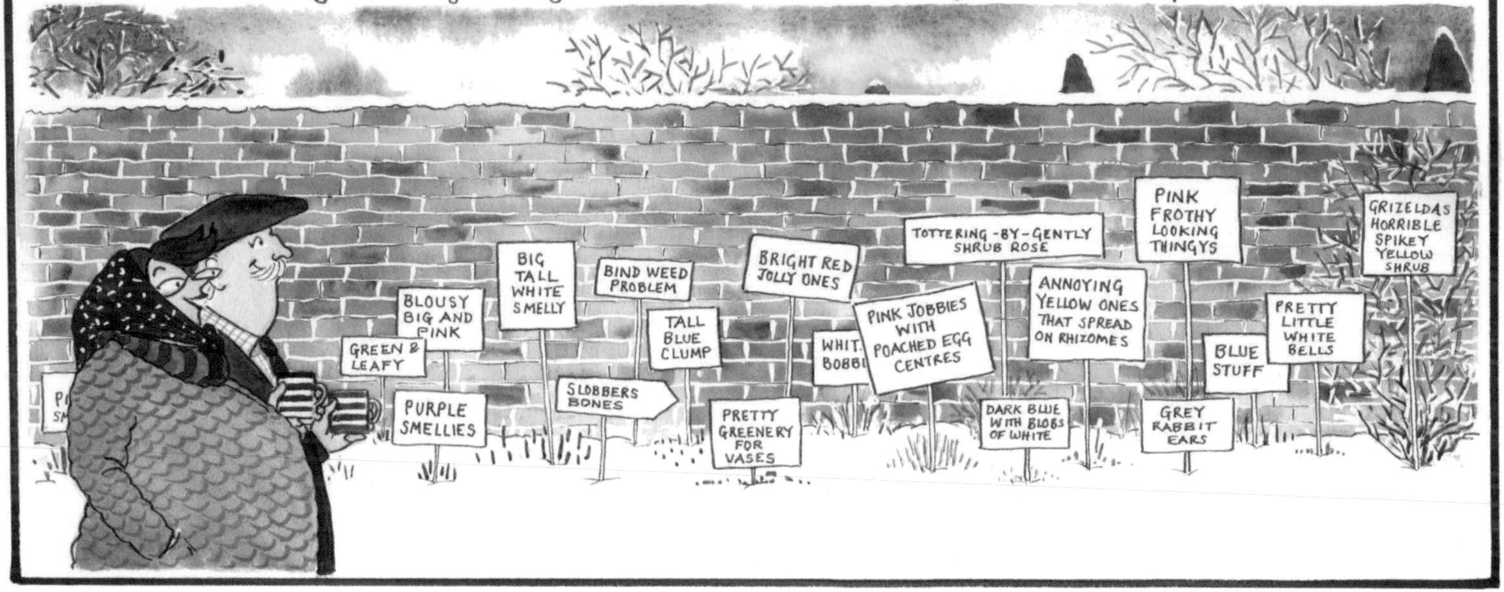

BIG TALL WHITE SMELLY
BIND WEED PROBLEM
BRIGHT RED JOLLY ONES
TOTTERING-BY-GENTLY SHRUB ROSE
PINK FROTHY LOOKING THINGYS
GRIZELDAS HORRIBLE SPIKEY YELLOW SHRUB
BLOUSY BIG AND PINK
GREEN & LEAFY
TALL BLUE CLUMP
PINK JOBBIES WITH POACHED EGG CENTRES
ANNOYING YELLOW ONES THAT SPREAD ON RHIZOMES
PRETTY LITTLE WHITE BELLS
BLUE STUFF
SLOBBERS BONES
PURPLE SMELLIES
PRETTY GREENERY FOR VASES
DARK BLUE WITH BLOBS OF WHITE
GREY RABBIT EARS

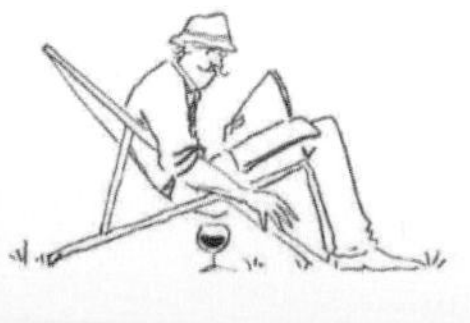

Of course I remembered it was your birthday!

I've prepared a wonderful dentally friendly lunch al fresco for you...

Just remove the cork...

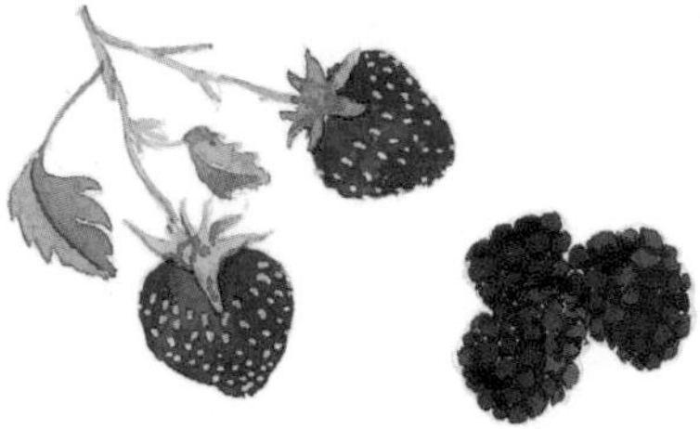

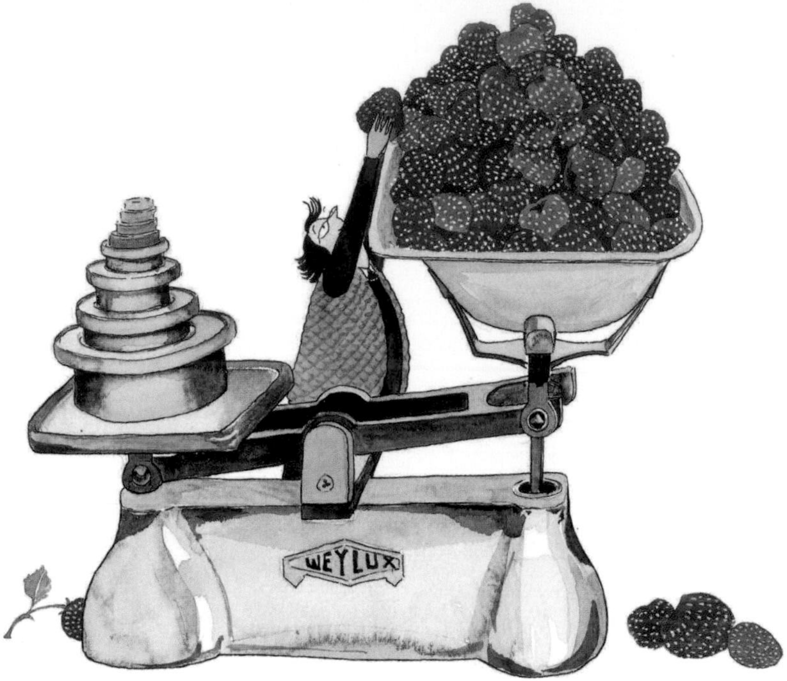
WEYLUX

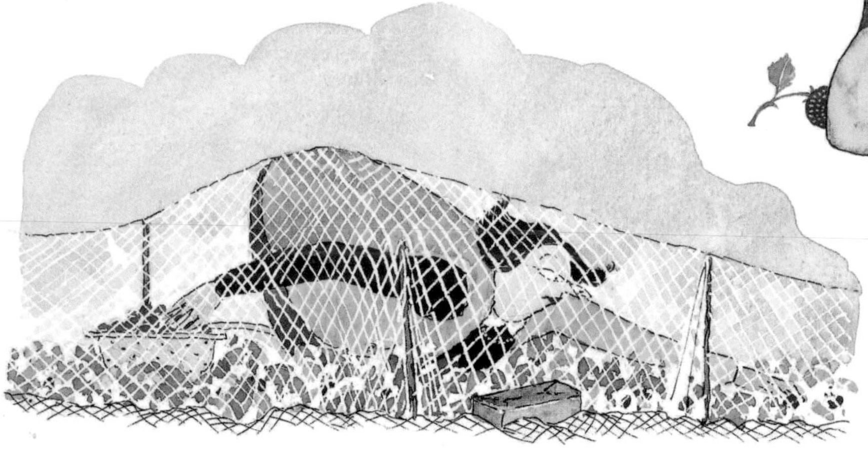

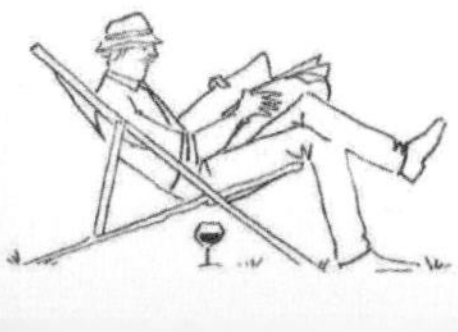

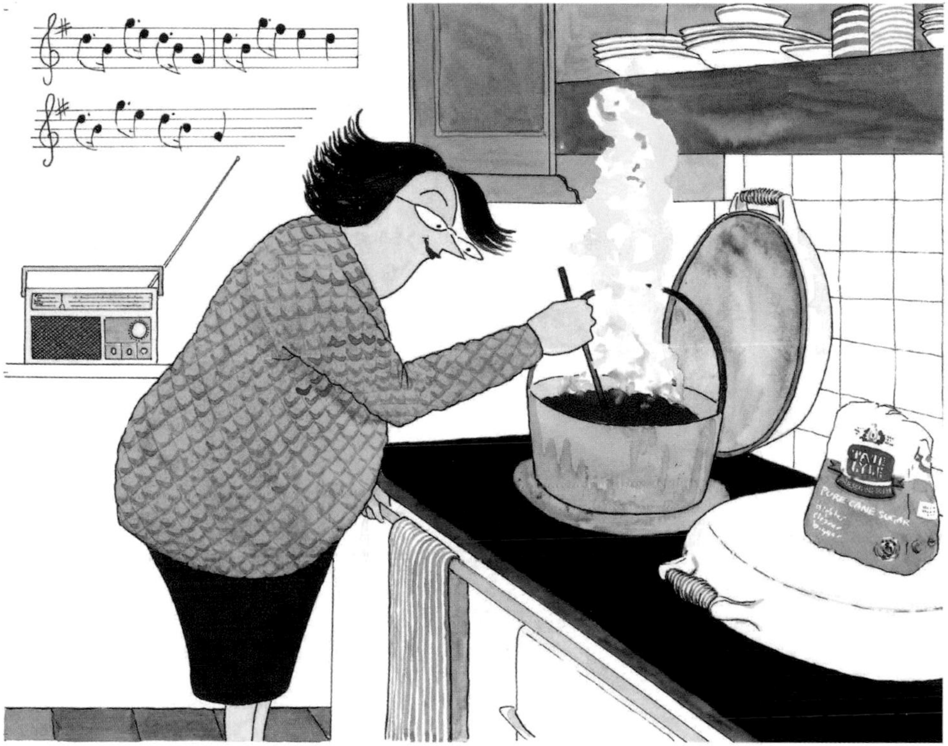

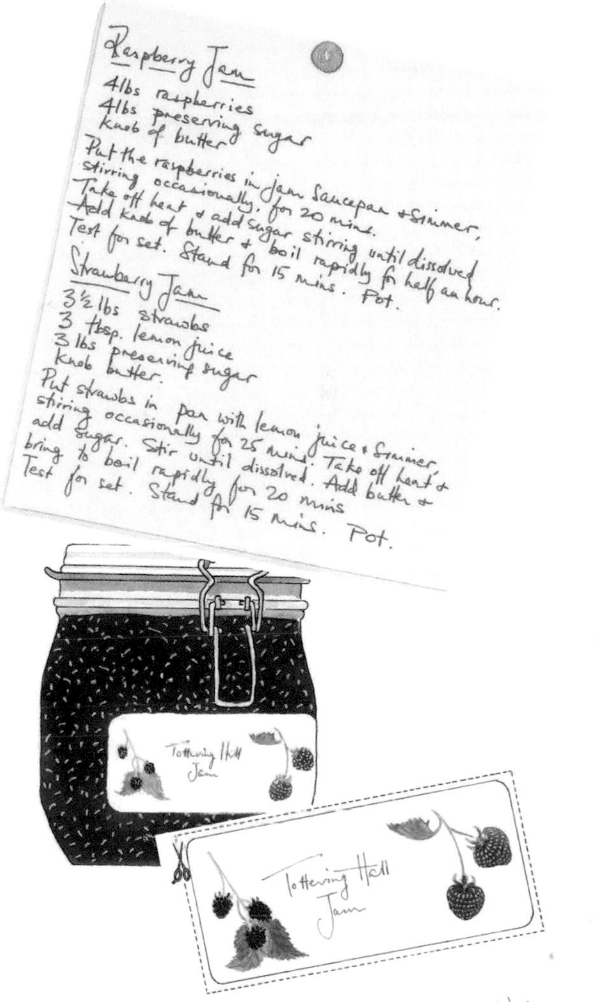
Raspberry Jam
4lbs raspberries
4lbs preserving sugar
Knob of butter
Put the raspberries in jam saucepan & simmer, stirring occasionally, for 20 mins.
Take off heat & add sugar stirring until dissolved
Add knob of butter & boil rapidly for half an hour.
Test for set. Stand for 15 mins. Pot.
Strawberry Jam
3½ lbs strawbs
3 tbsp. lemon juice
3 lbs preserving sugar
Knob butter.
Put strawbs in pan with lemon juice & simmer, stirring occasionally for 25 mins. Take off heat & add sugar. Stir until dissolved. Add butter & bring to boil rapidly for 20 mins
Test for set. Stand for 15 mins. Pot.
Tottering Hall Jam
Tottering Hall Jam

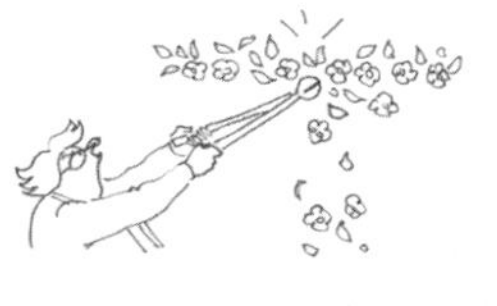

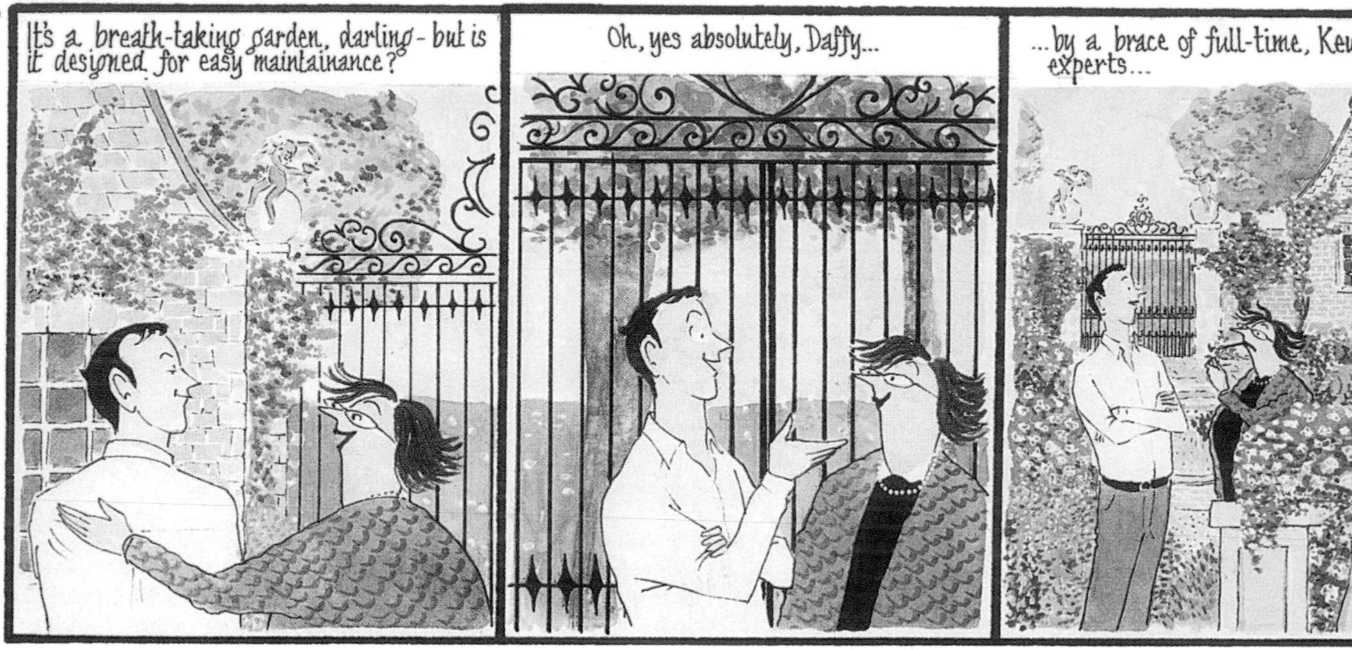
It's a breath-taking garden, darling - but is it designed for easy maintainance?
Oh, yes absolutely, Daffy...
...by a brace of full-time, Kew-trained experts...

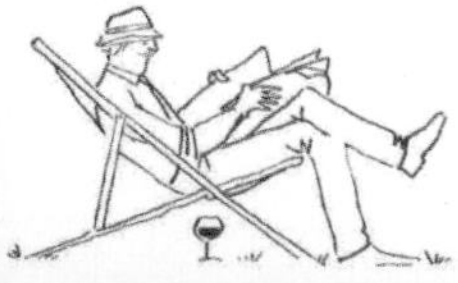

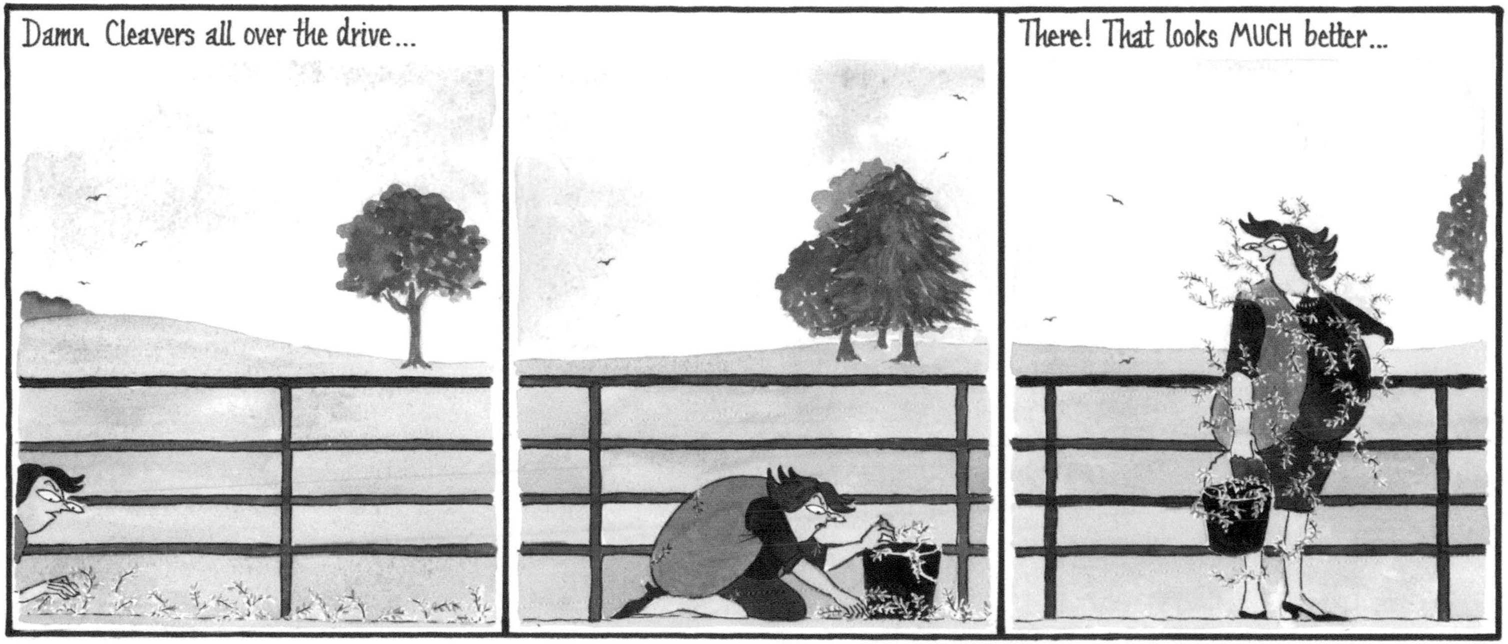
Damn. Cleavers all over the drive...
There! That looks MUCH better...

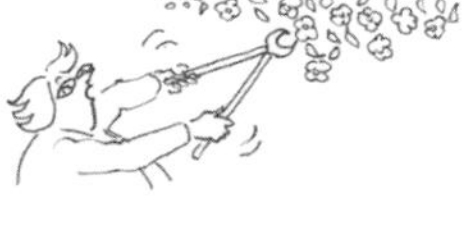

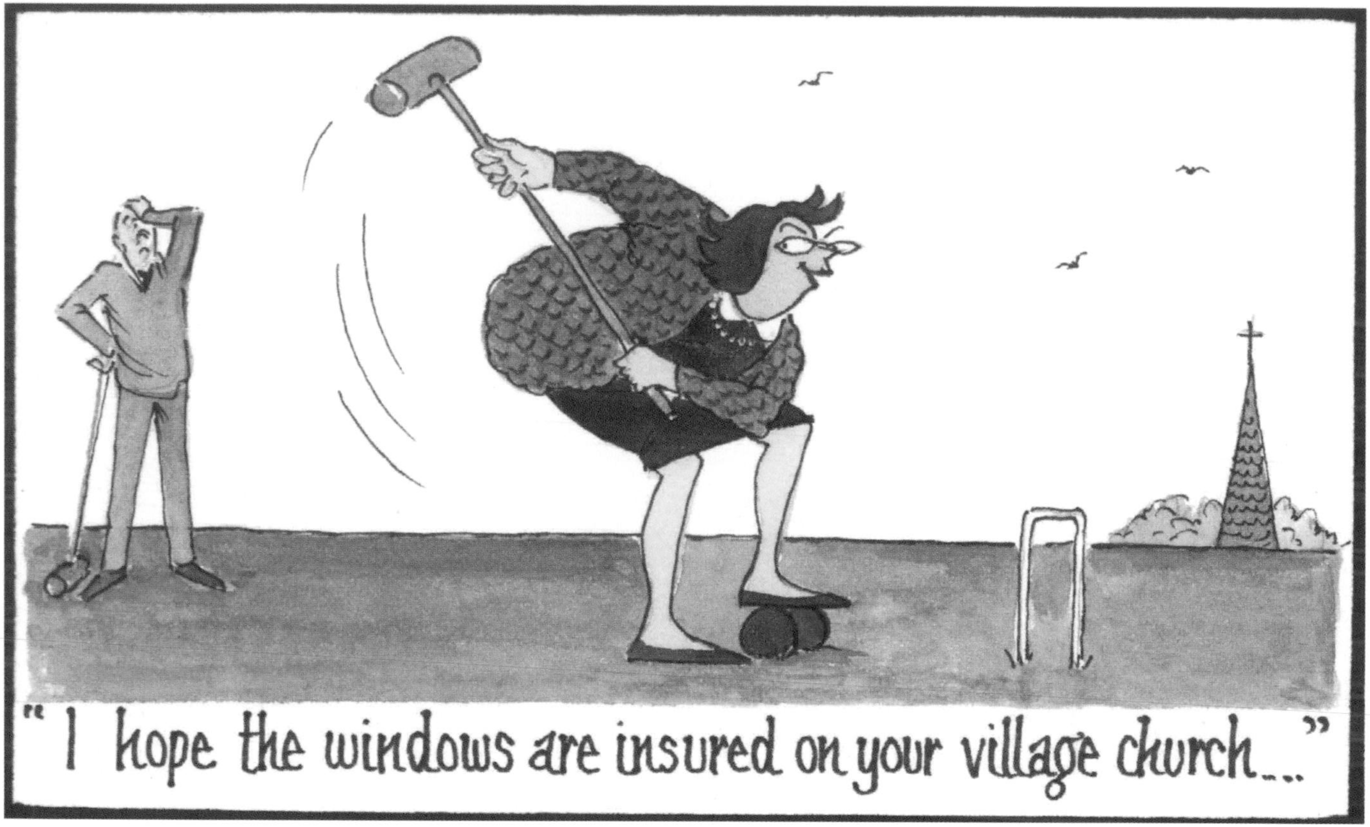

"I hope the windows are insured on your village church..."

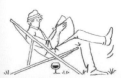

Oh! Dear! Another Daisy must have come up on the lawn...

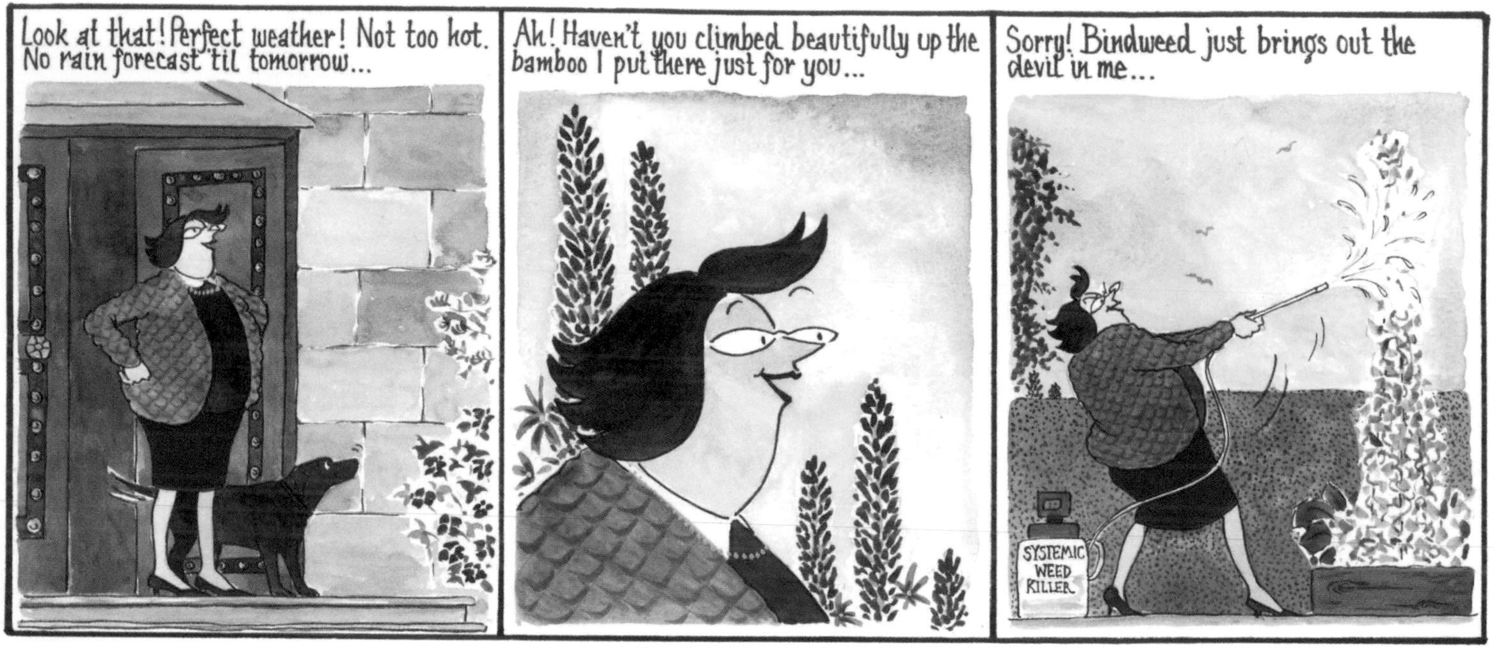
Look at that! Perfect weather! Not too hot. No rain forecast 'til tomorrow...
Ah! Haven't you climbed beautifully up the bamboo I put there just for you...
Sorry! Bindweed just brings out the devil in me...
SYSTEMIC WEED KILLER

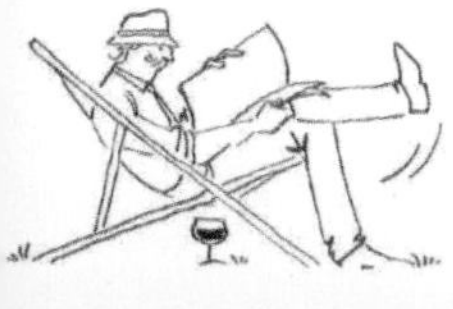

You need a good strong pesticide to kill off those caterpillars, darling...
That's a disgraceful suggestion, Colin! I use a totally organic alternative...
... the foot...
squish!

PLEASE DRIVE CAREFULLY!
GRANDPARENTS VISITING!

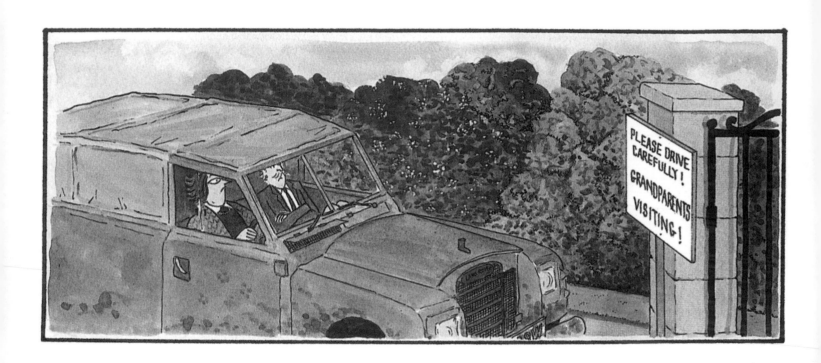

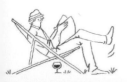

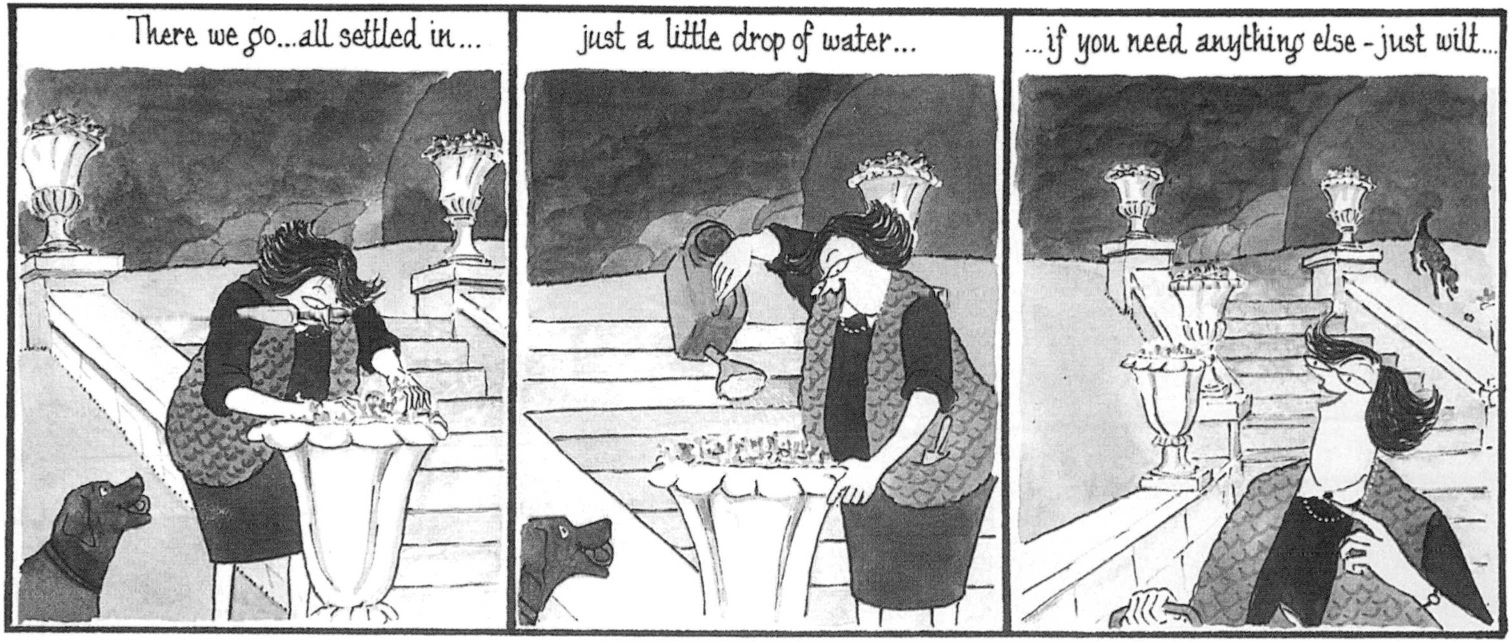
There we go...all settled in...
just a little drop of water...
...if you need anything else - just wilt...

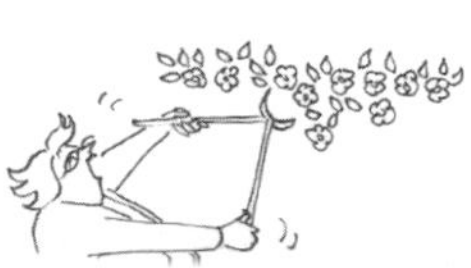

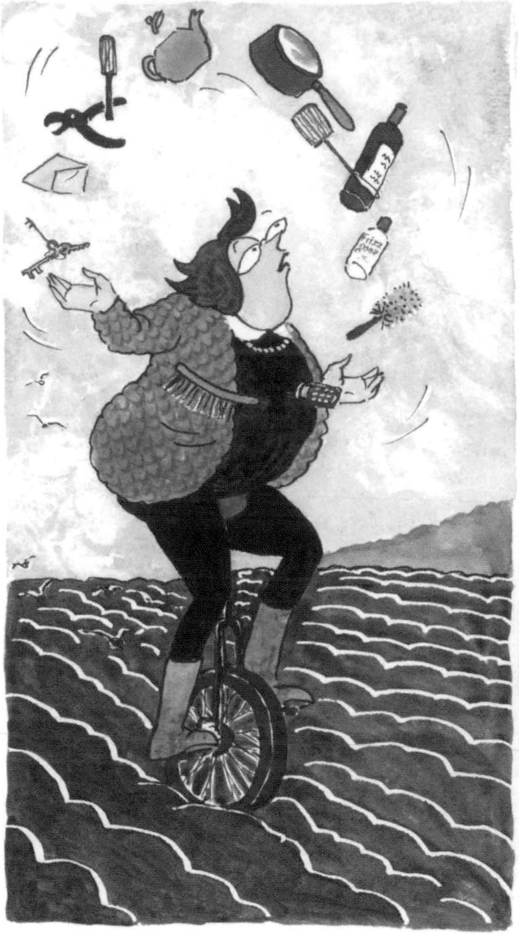

A woman's life can feel like performing a juggling act whilst riding a unicycle through a ploughed field...

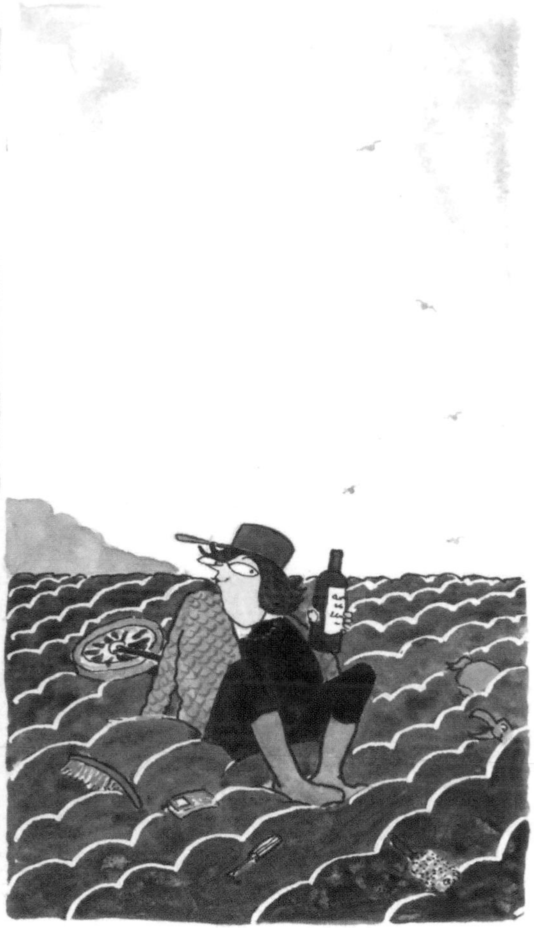

Sometimes we just have to prioritise...

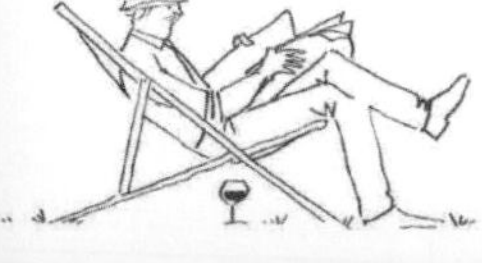

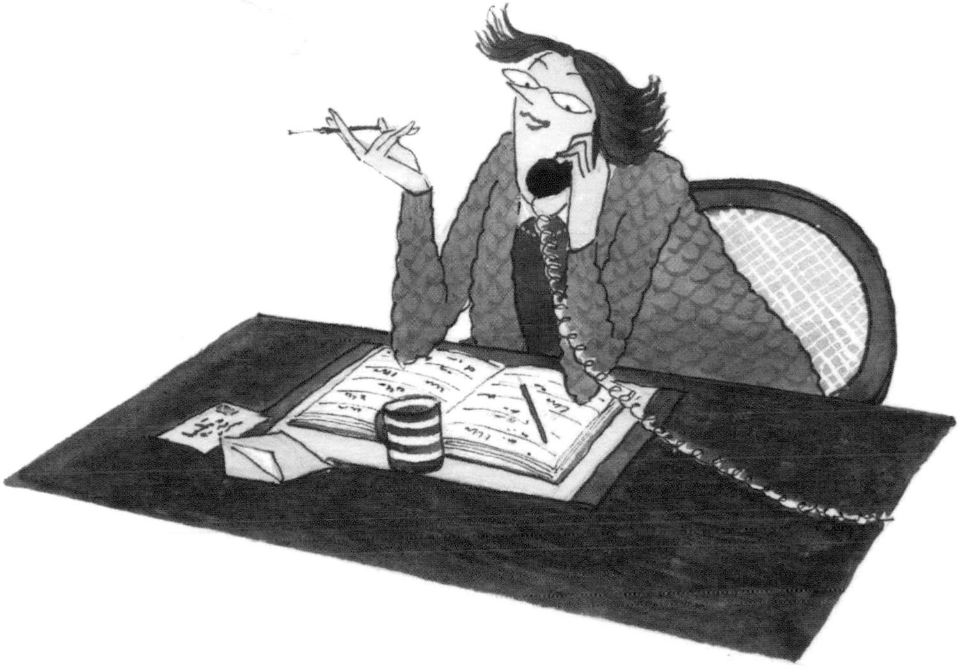

"... and when you've done the herbaceous border, could you remember to prune my Ascot hat ..."

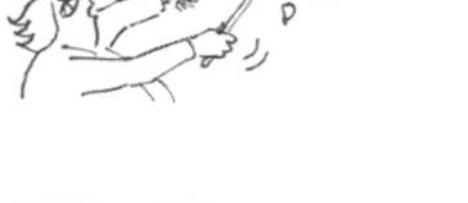

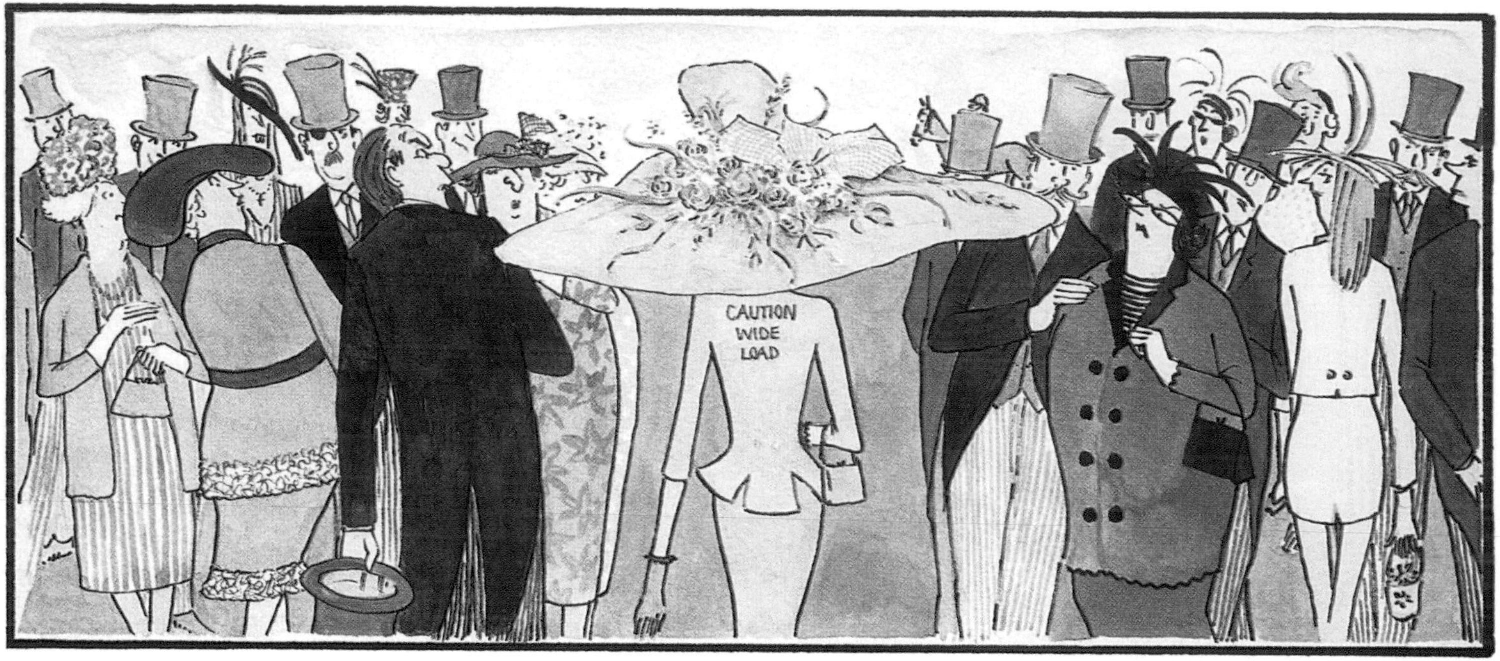
CAUTION
WIDE
LOAD

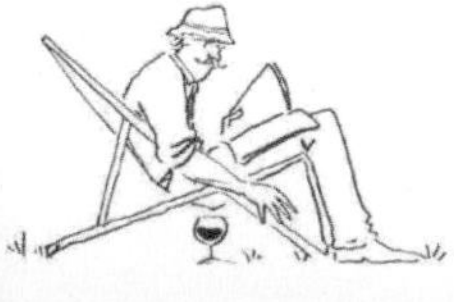

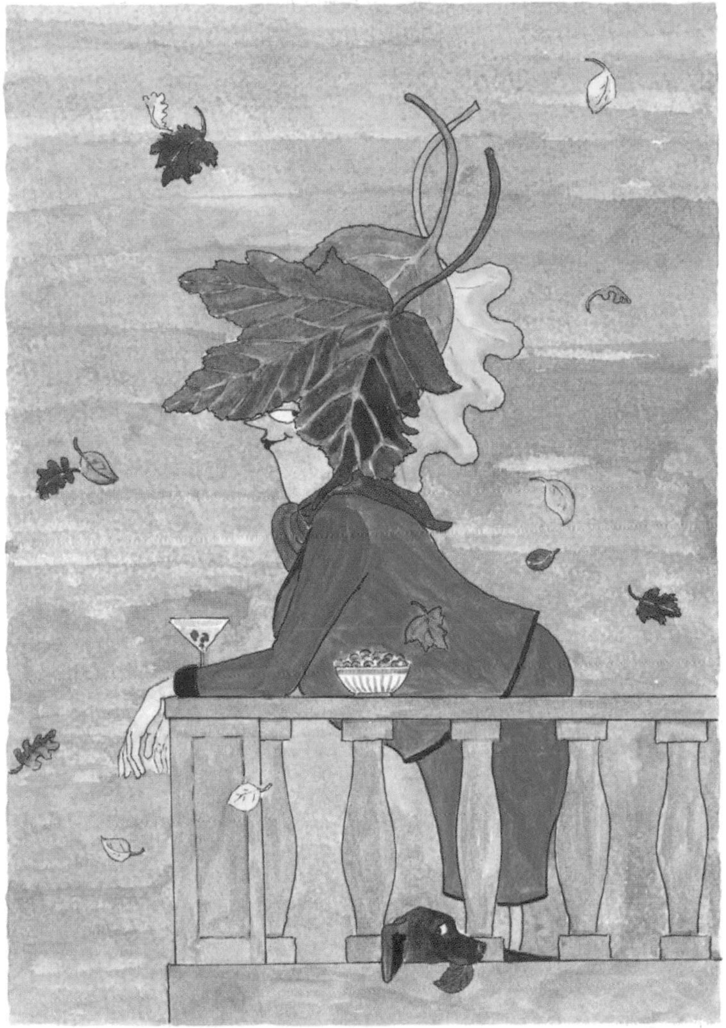

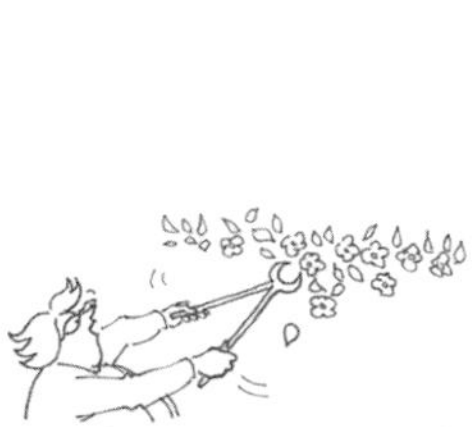

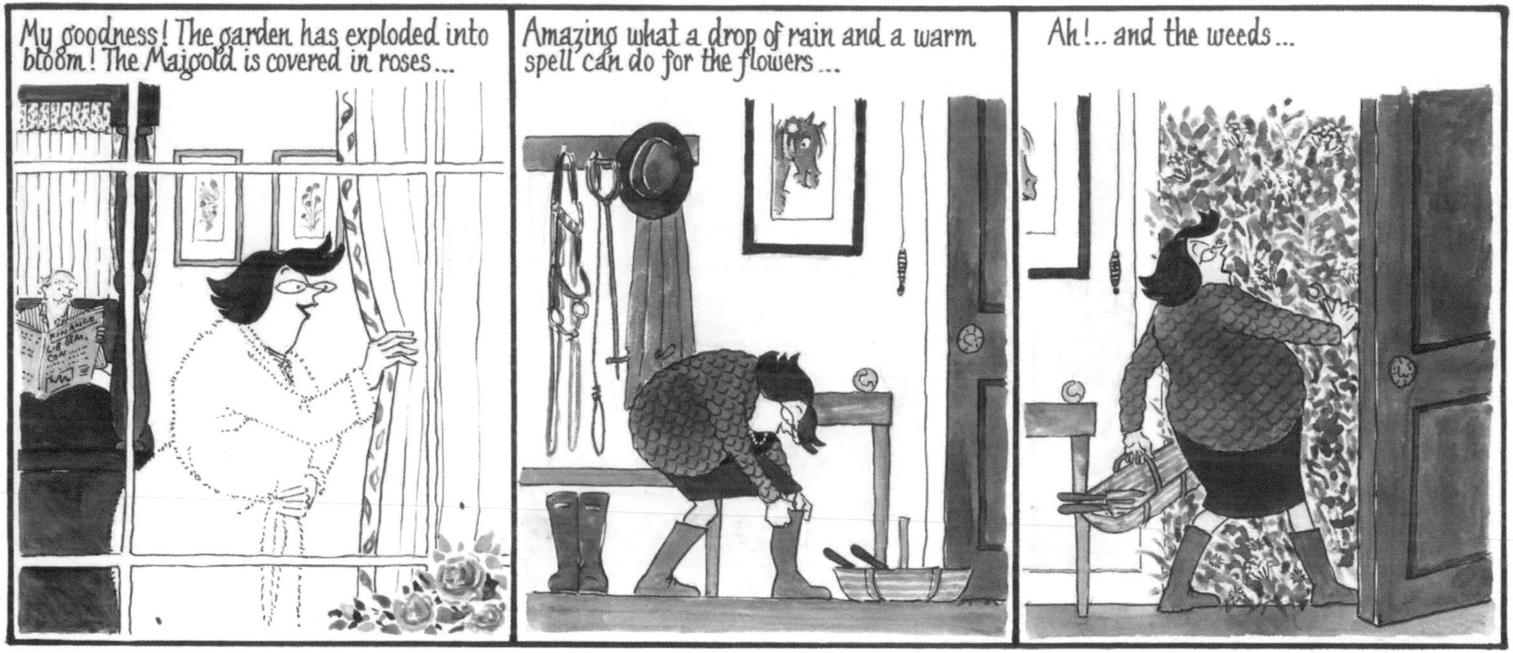
My goodness! The garden has exploded into bloom! The Maigold is covered in roses...
Amazing what a drop of rain and a warm spell can do for the flowers...
Ah!.. and the weeds...

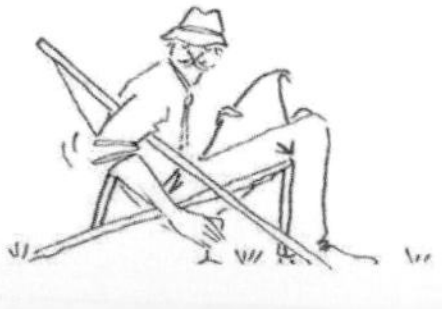

Our first organic carrot Dicky...

Daffy Prepares for Battle

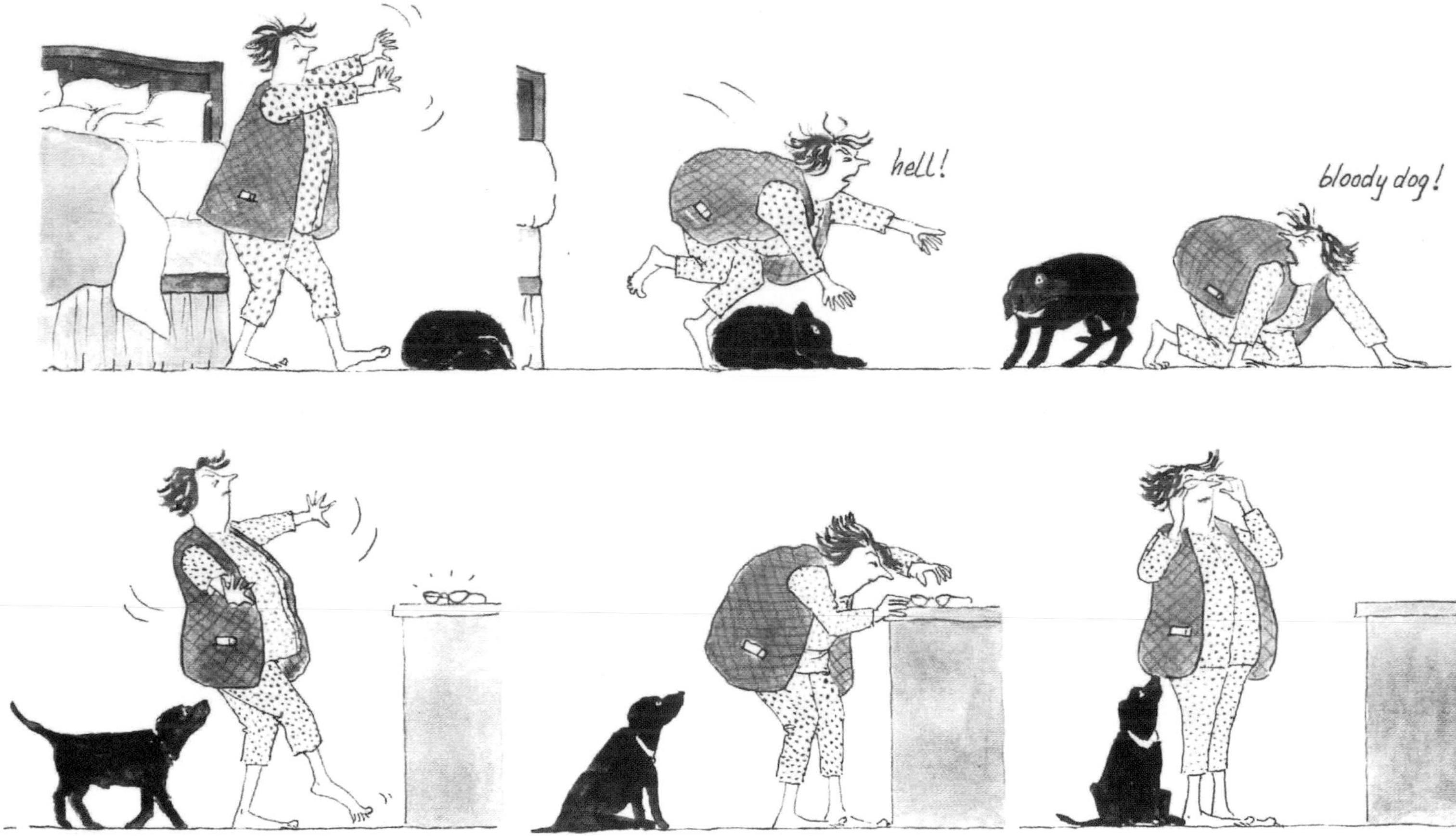
hell!
bloody dog!

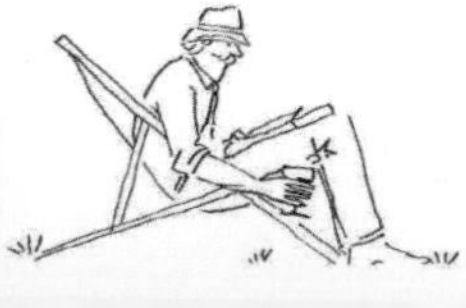

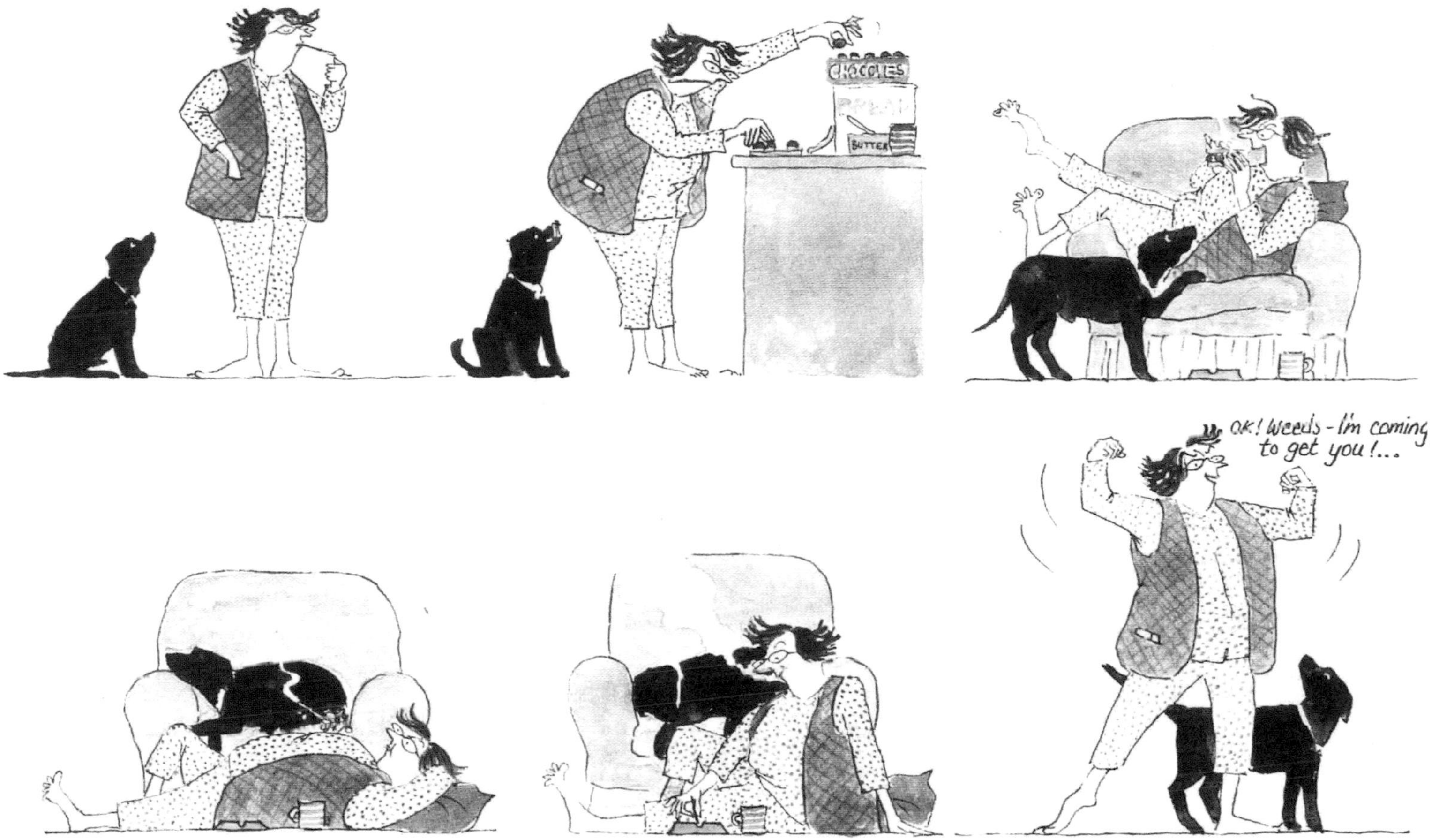
BUTTER
OK! Weeds - I'm coming to get you!...

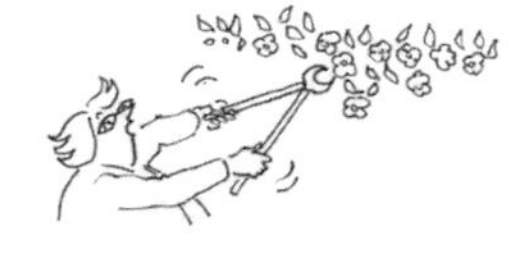

I think Mum's finally lost the plot with the ground Elder...

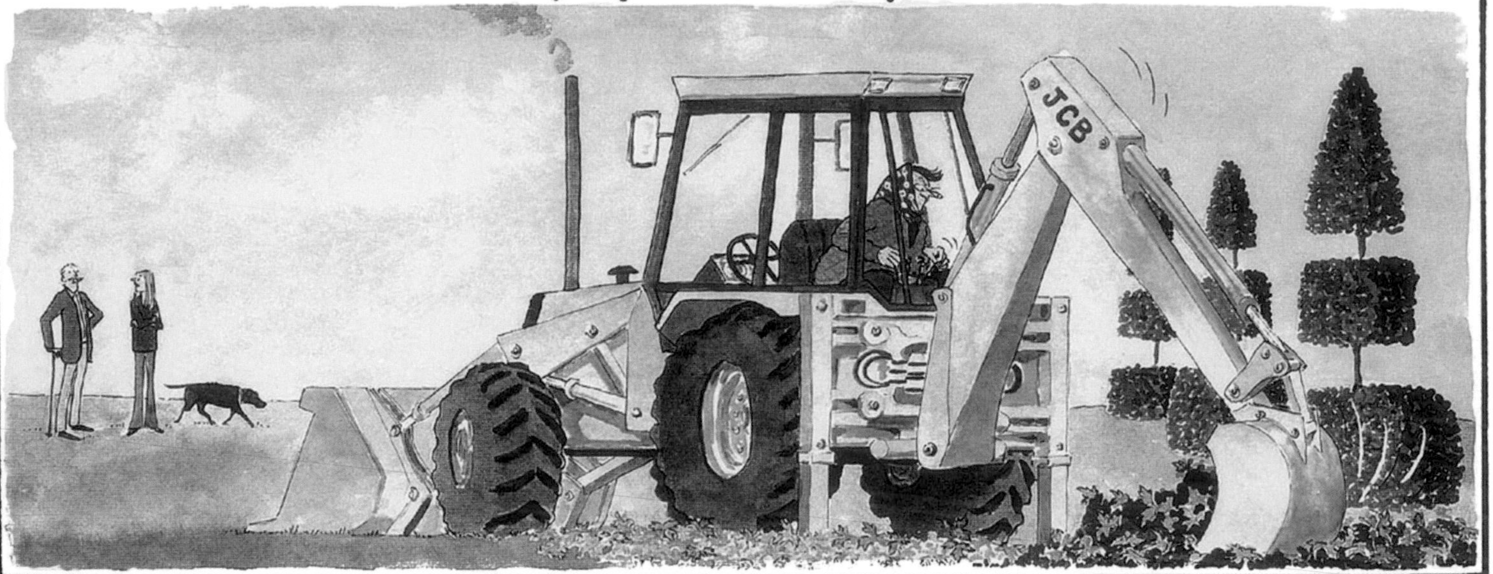
JCB

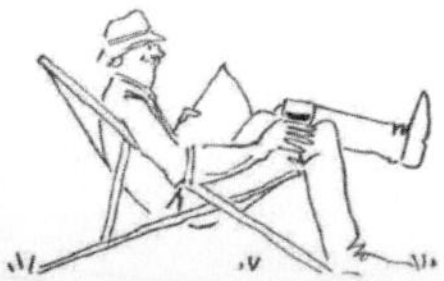

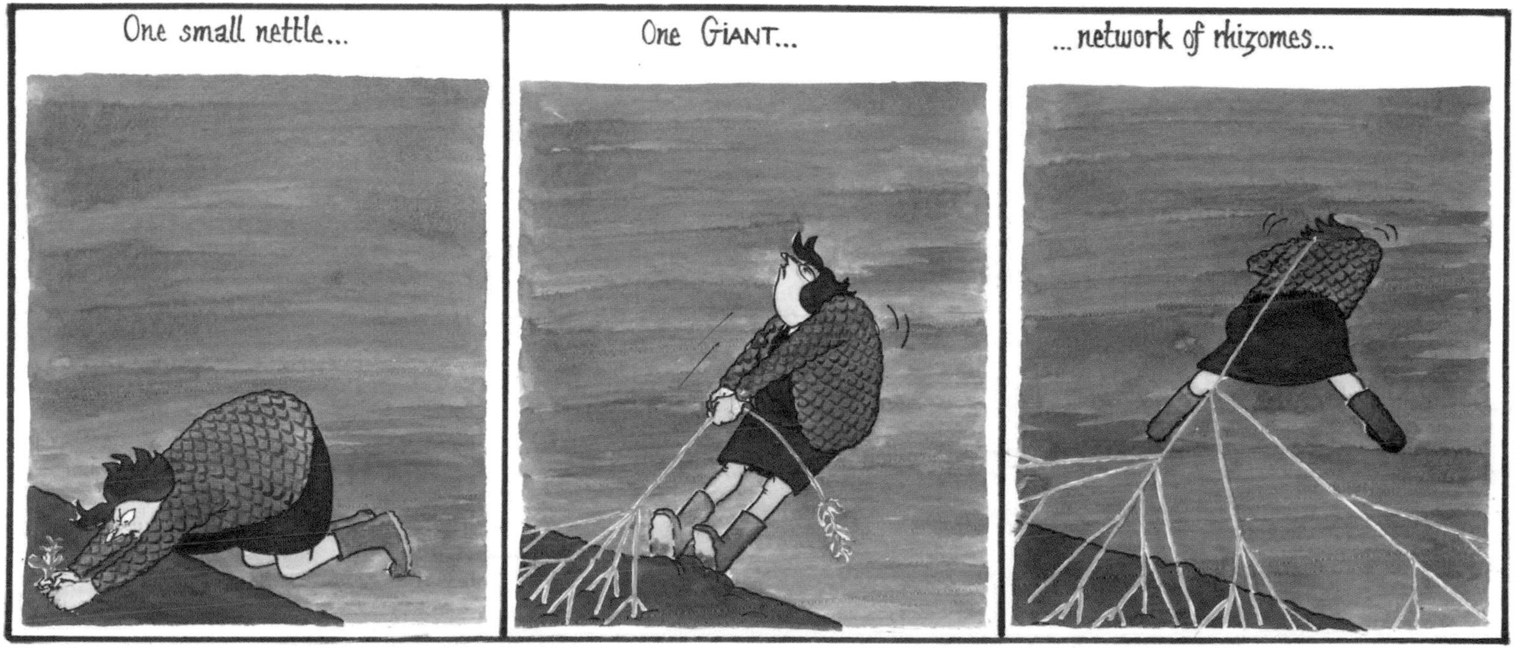
One small nettle...
One GIANT...
...network of rhizomes...

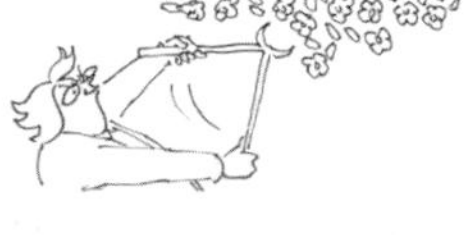

"Are you sure you didn't mean 'Ground Elder shall inherit the earth?'..."

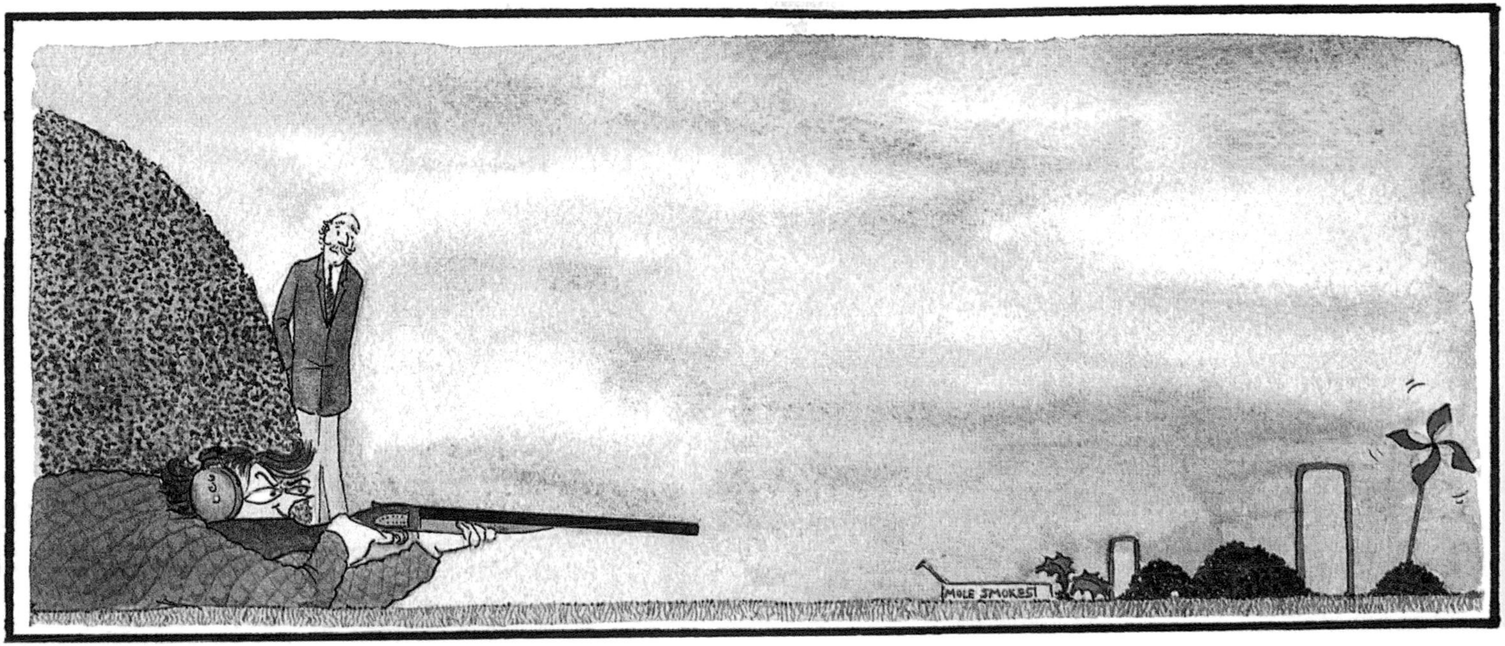
MOLE SMOKES!

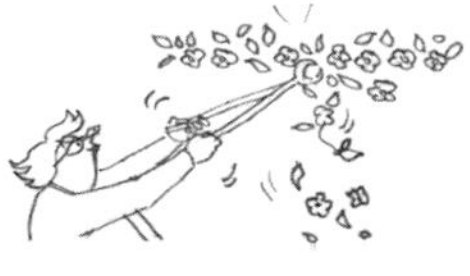

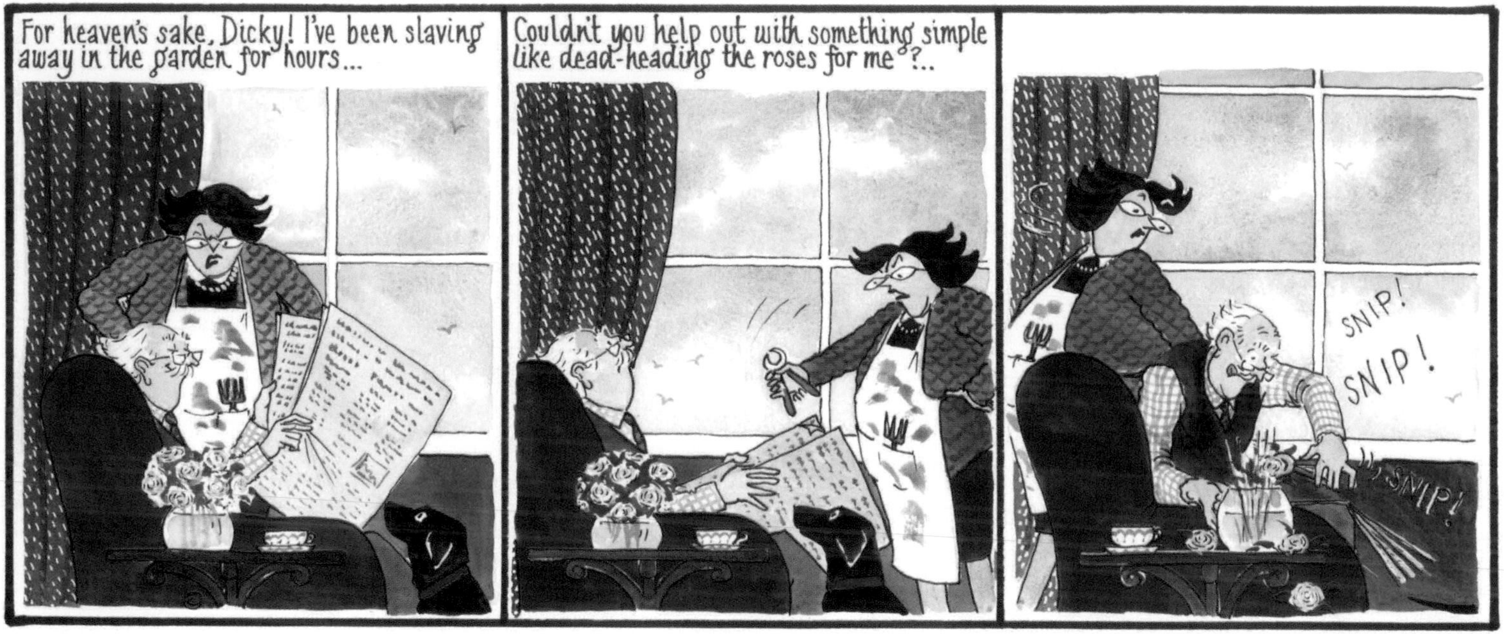
For heaven's sake, Dicky! I've been slaving away in the garden for hours...
Couldn't you help out with something simple like dead-heading the roses for me?..
SNIP!
SNIP!
SNIP!

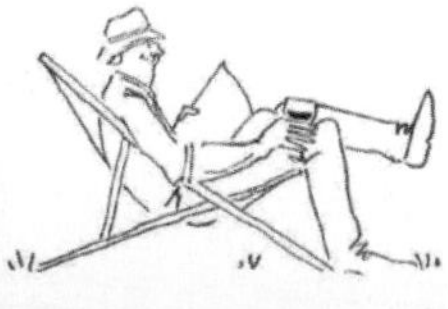

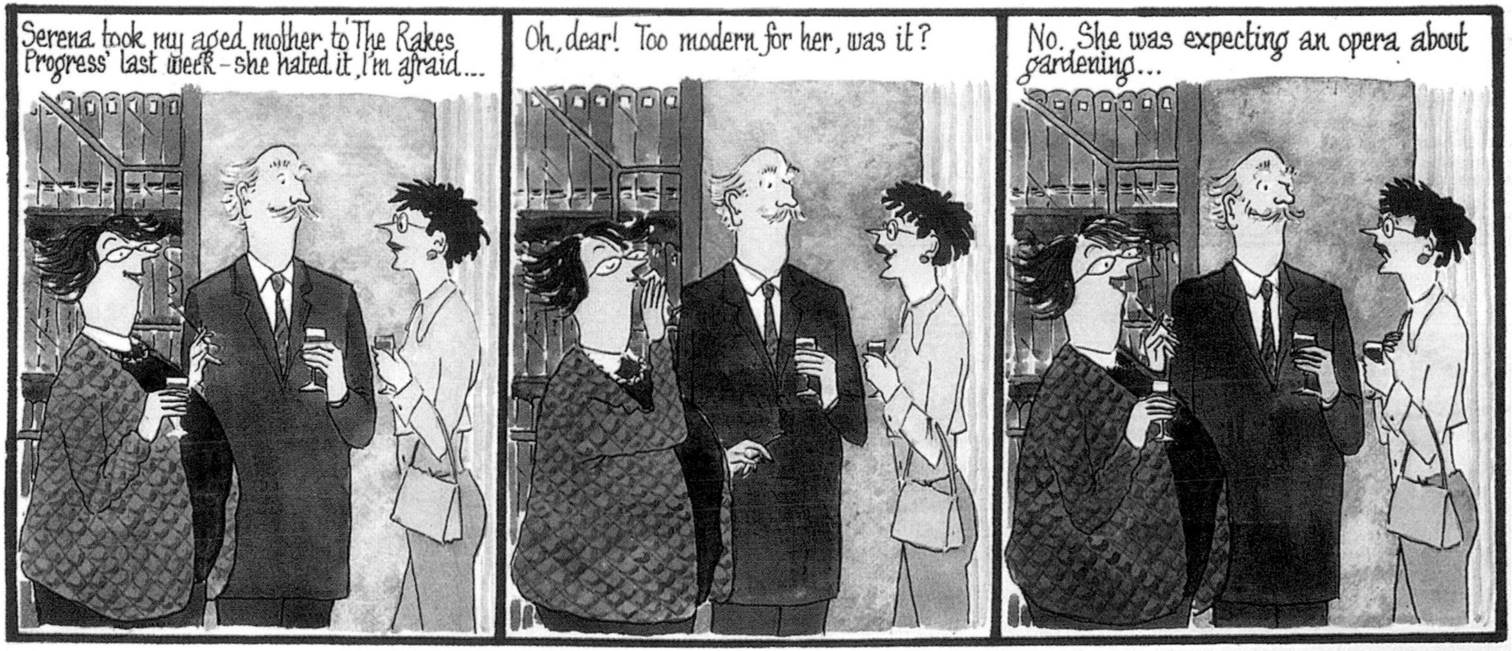
Serena took my aged mother to 'The Rakes Progress' last week – she hated it, I'm afraid....
Oh, dear! Too modern for her, was it?
No. She was expecting an opera about gardening...

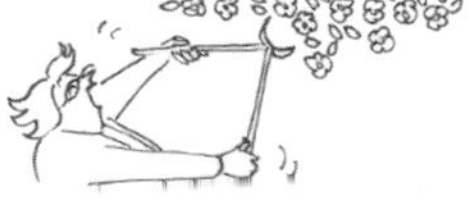

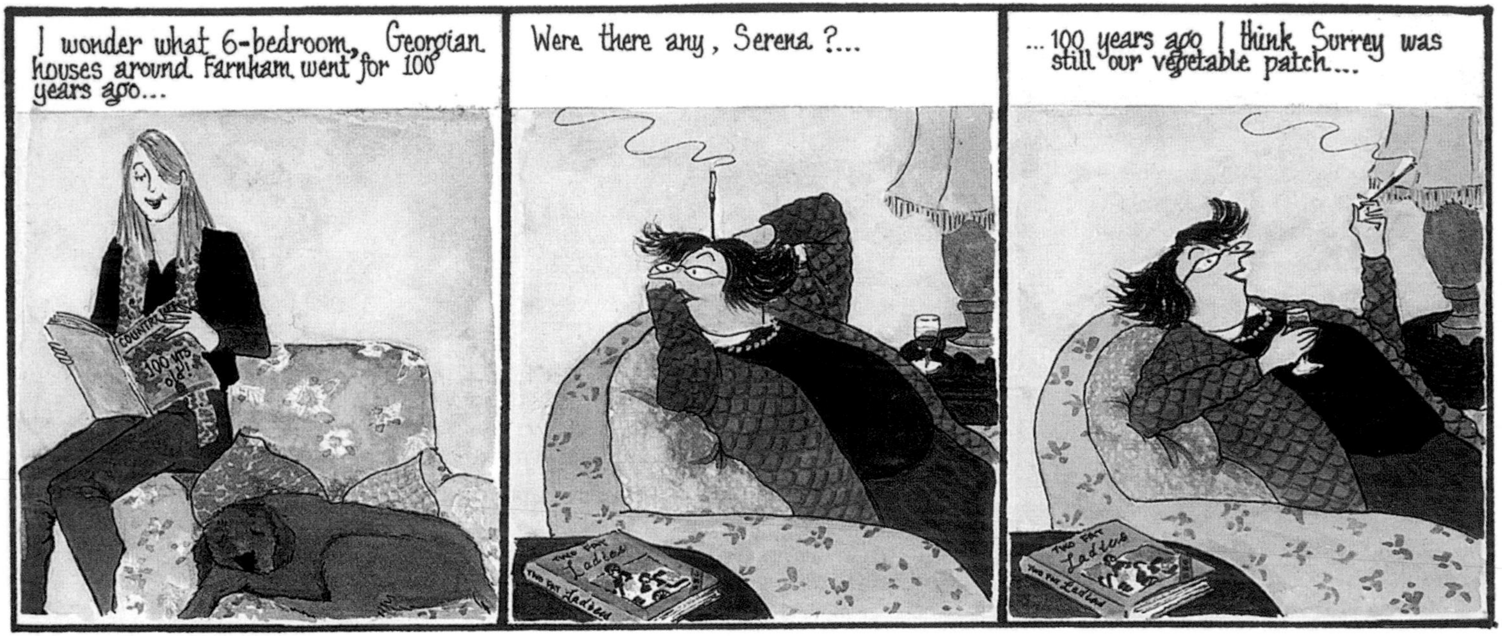
I wonder what 6-bedroom, Georgian houses around Farnham went for 100 years ago...
100 yrs old!
Were there any, Serena ?...
Two Fat Ladies
... 100 years ago I think Surrey was still our vegetable patch...
Two Fat Ladies

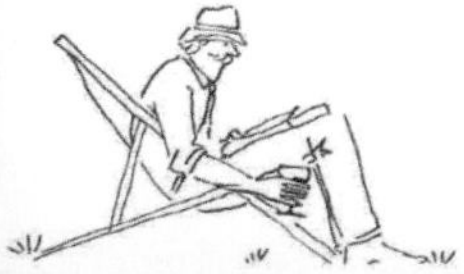

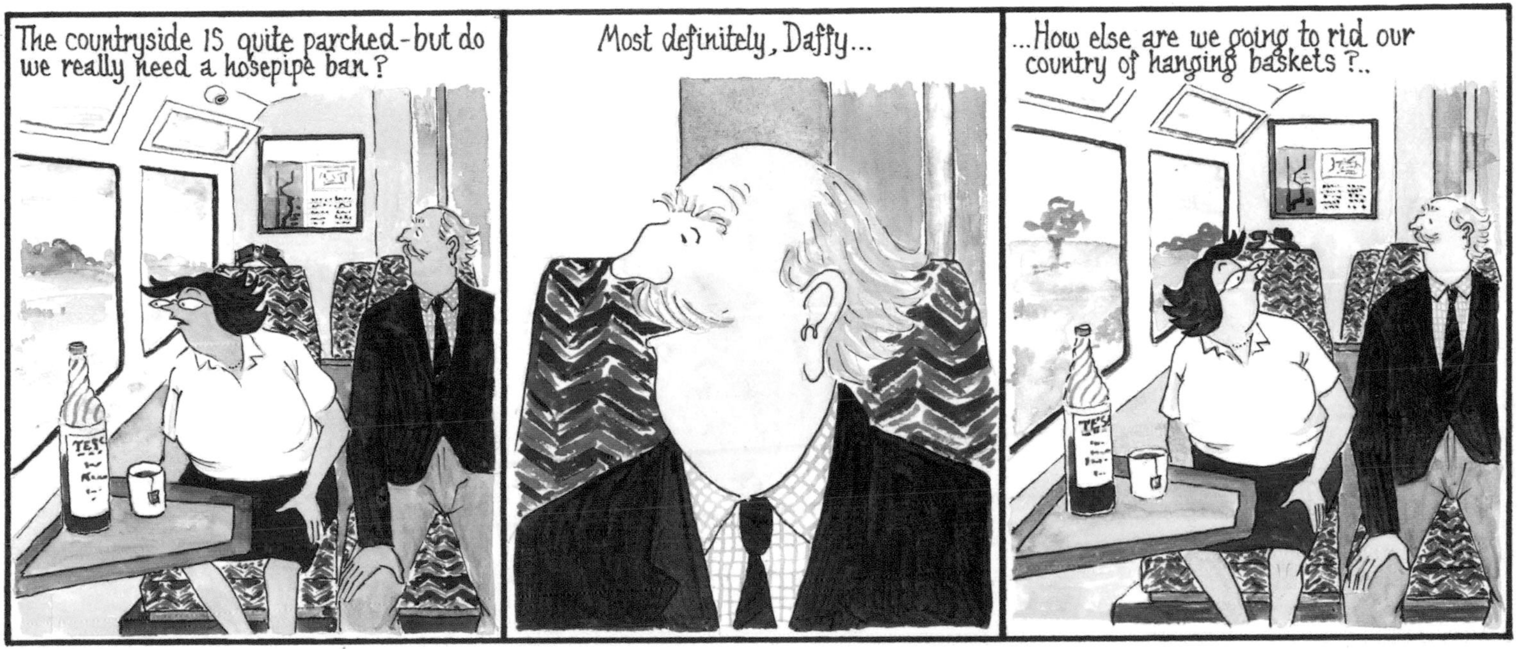
The countryside IS quite parched - but do we really need a hosepipe ban?
Most definitely, Daffy...
...How else are we going to rid our country of hanging baskets?..

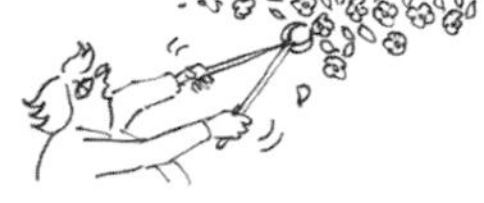

FLOWER SHOW VISITOR
The hardy perennial

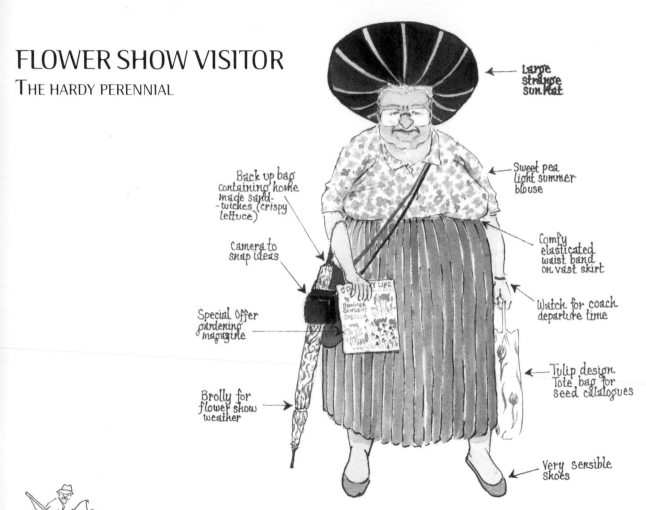

Large strange sun hat

Sweet pea light summer blouse

Comfy elasticated waist band on vast skirt

Watch for coach departure time

Tulip design tote bag for seed catalogues

Very sensible shoes

Back up bag containing home made sand--wiches (crispy lettuce)

Camera to snap ideas

Special offer gardening magazine

Brolly for flower show weather

Miss Buffy Tip-Moth

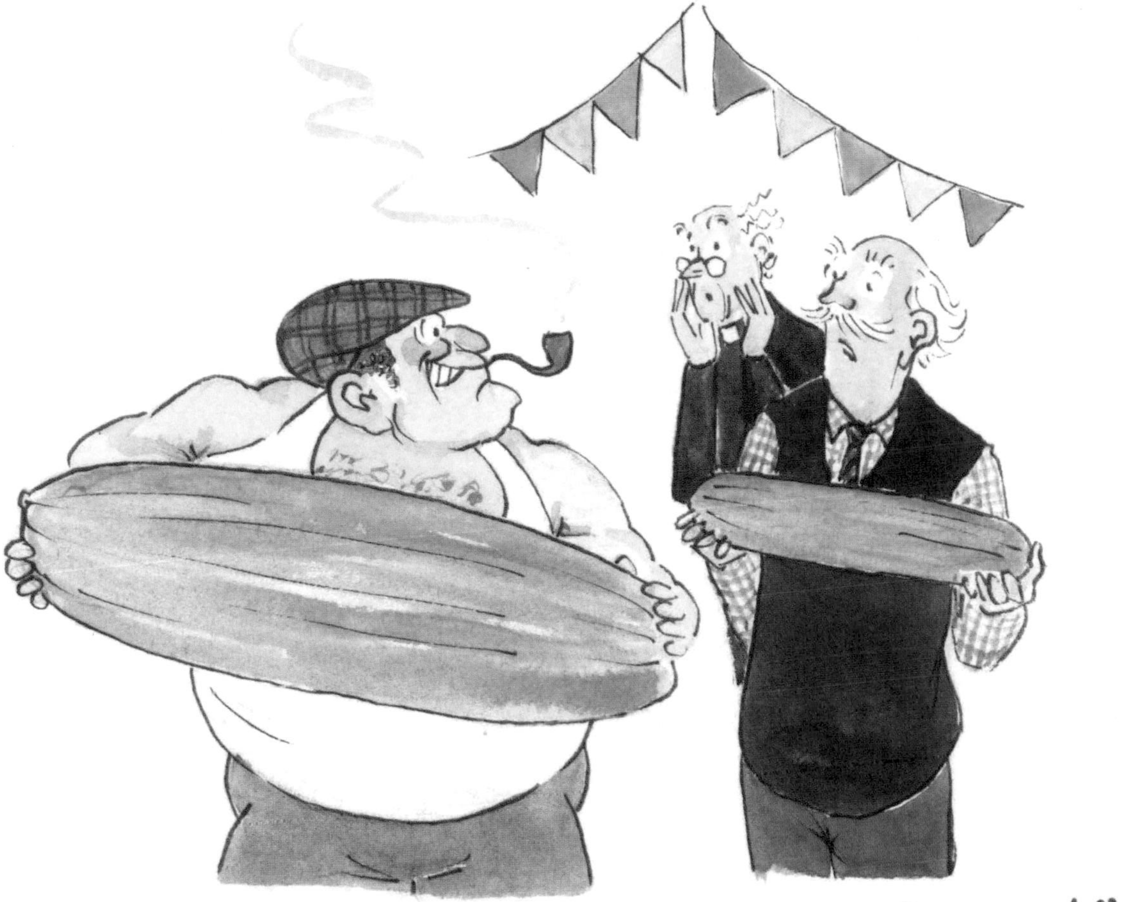

"Wow! You've certainly got a whopper!"

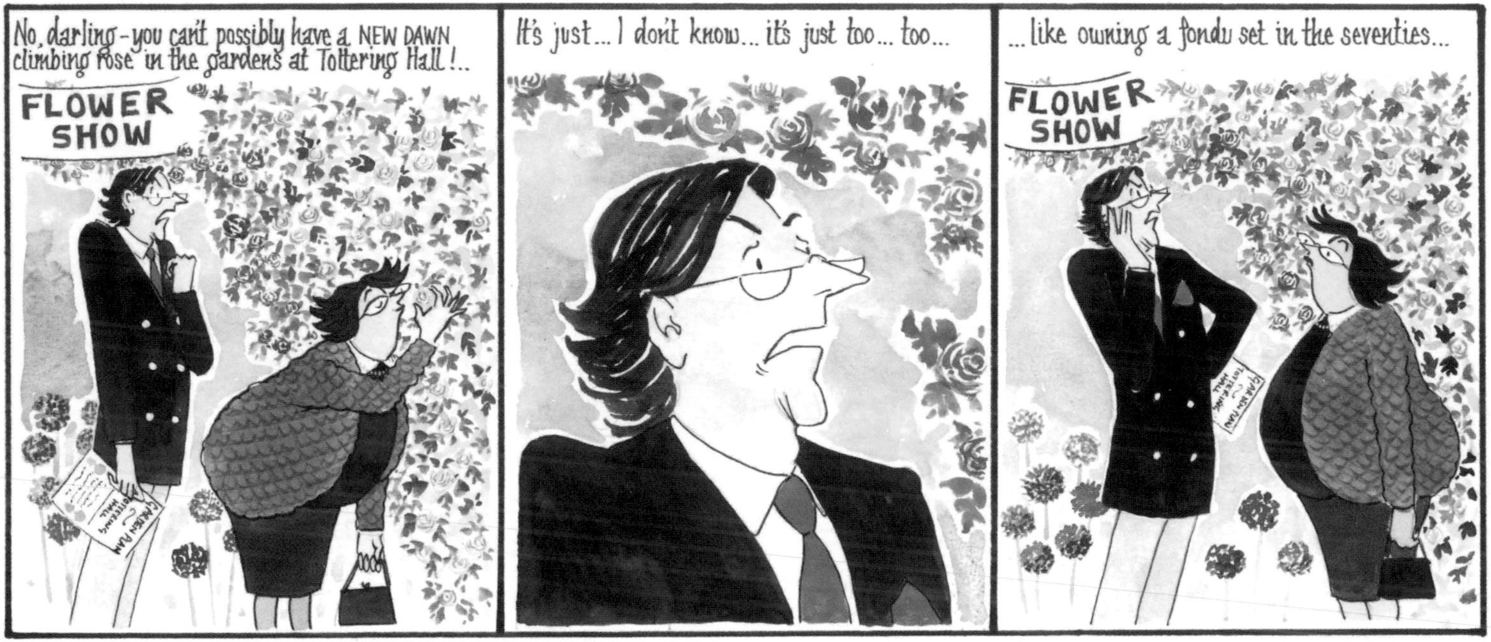
No, darling – you can't possibly have a NEW DAWN climbing rose in the gardens at Tottering Hall!..
FLOWER SHOW
It's just... I don't know... it's just too... too...
... like owning a fondu set in the seventies...
FLOWER SHOW

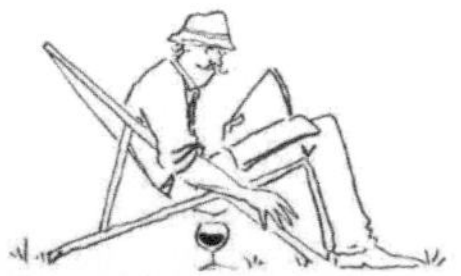

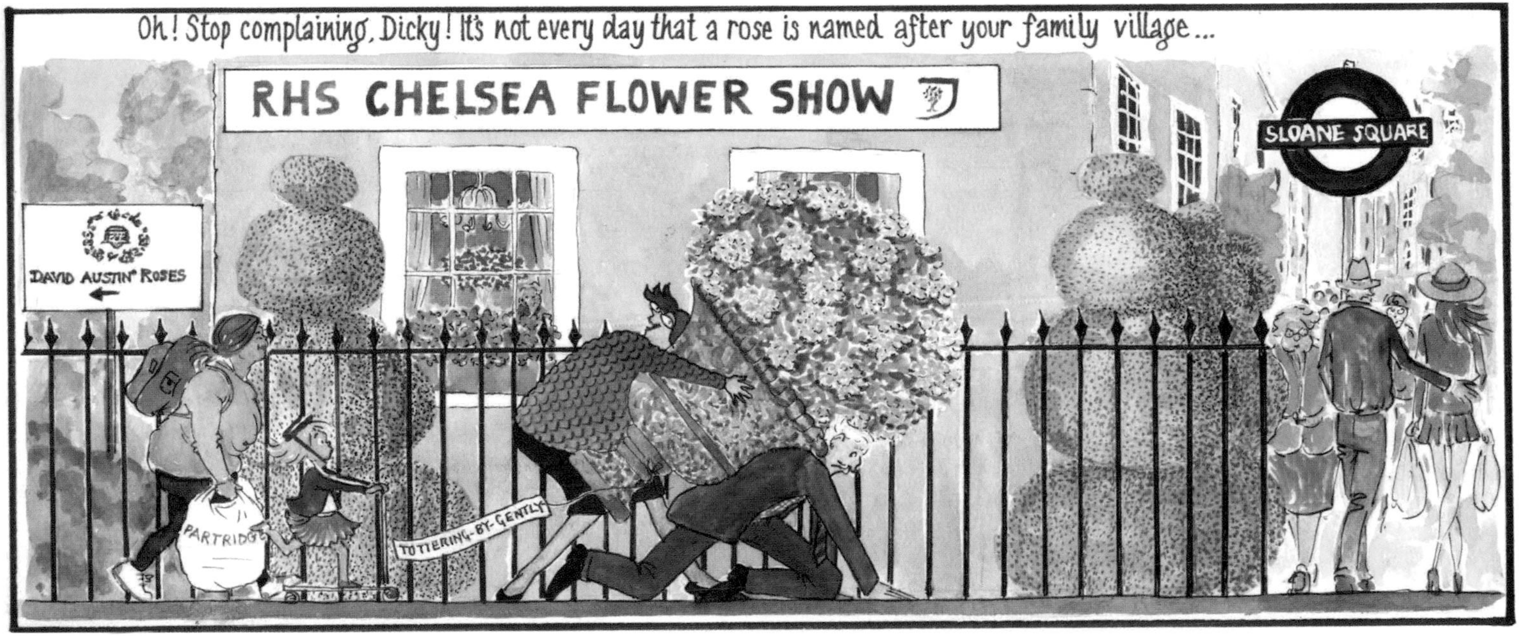
Oh! Stop complaining, Dicky! It's not every day that a rose is named after your family village...
RHS CHELSEA FLOWER SHOW
SLOANE SQUARE
DAVID AUSTIN® ROSES
PARTRIDGE
TOTTERING-BY-GENTLY

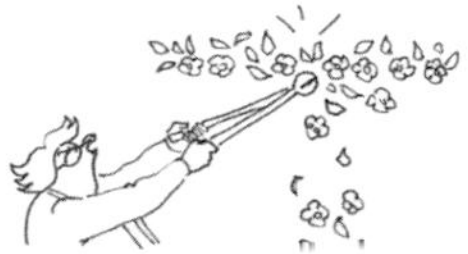

AN OLD POORLY SHAPED SPECIMEN...

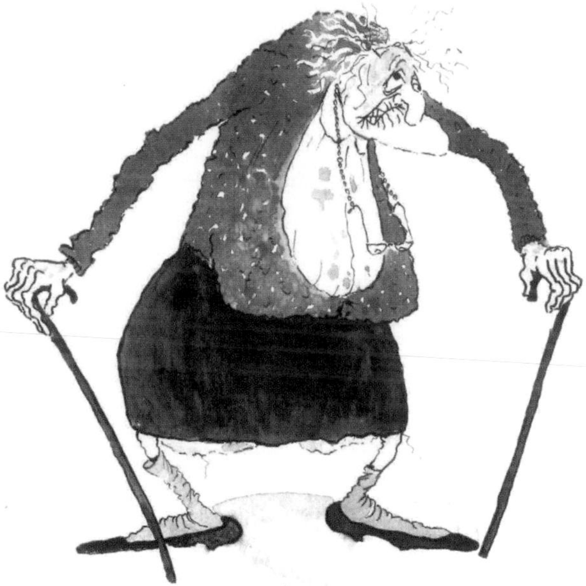

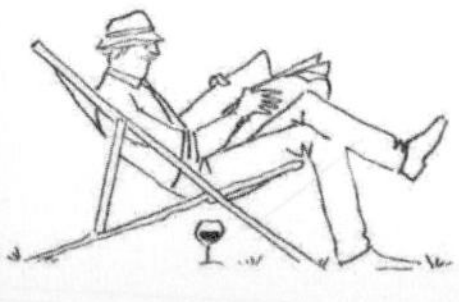

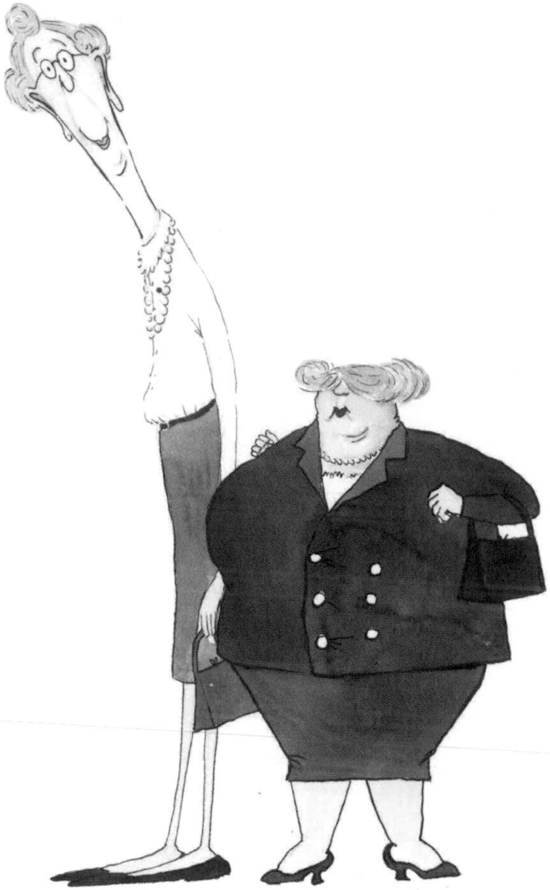

ARCHITECTURAL SHRUBS...

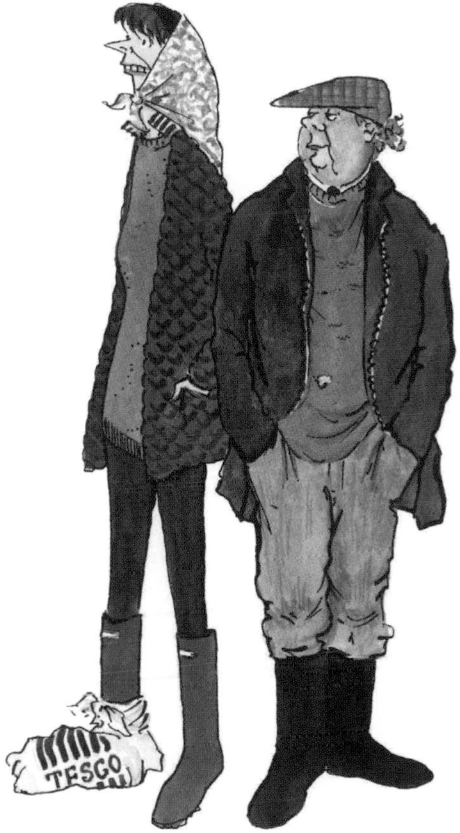
TESCO

Disappointing bedding varieties...

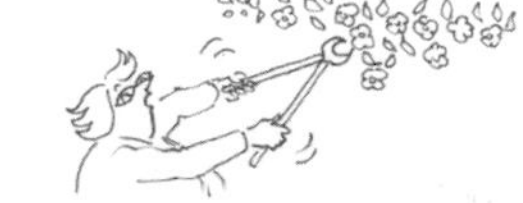

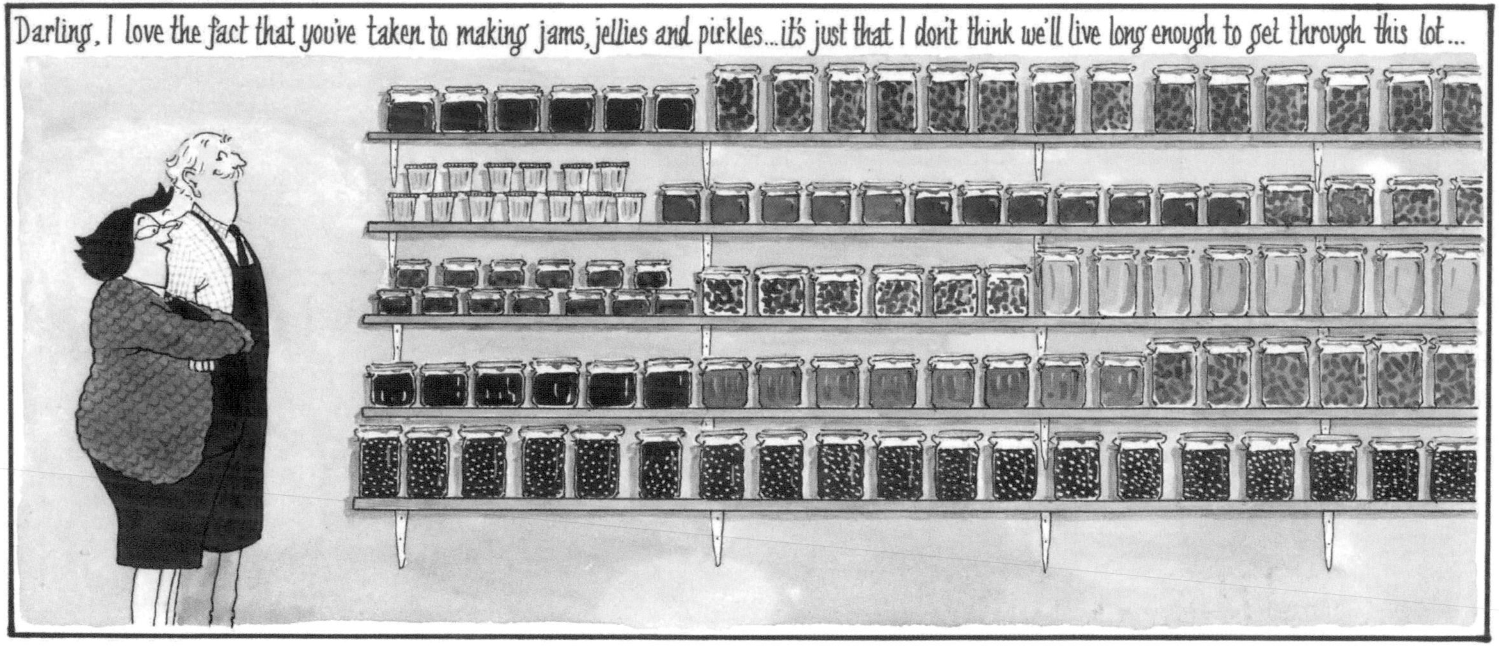
Darling, I love the fact that you've taken to making jams, jellies and pickles... it's just that I don't think we'll live long enough to get through this lot...

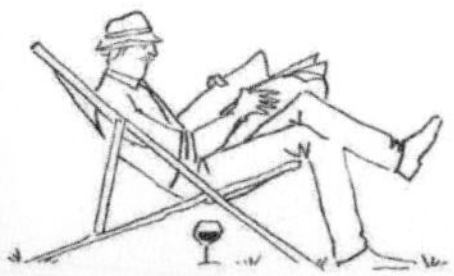

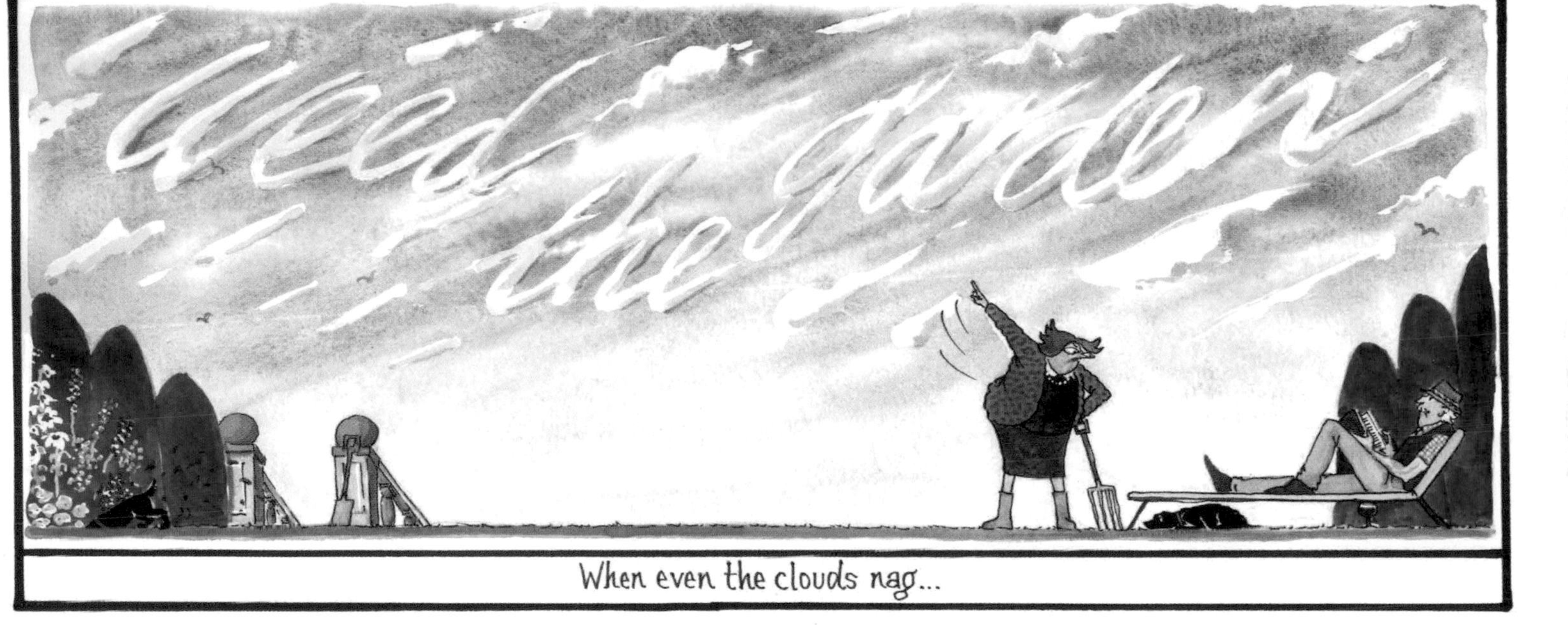
Weed the garden
When even the clouds nag...

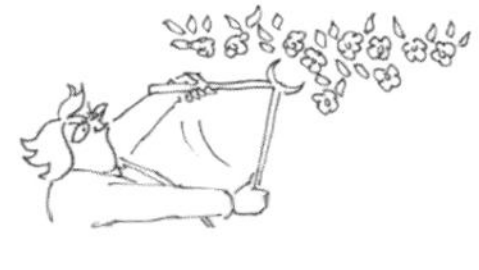

THE IMPORTANCE OF GETTING THE WHOLE TAP ROOT...

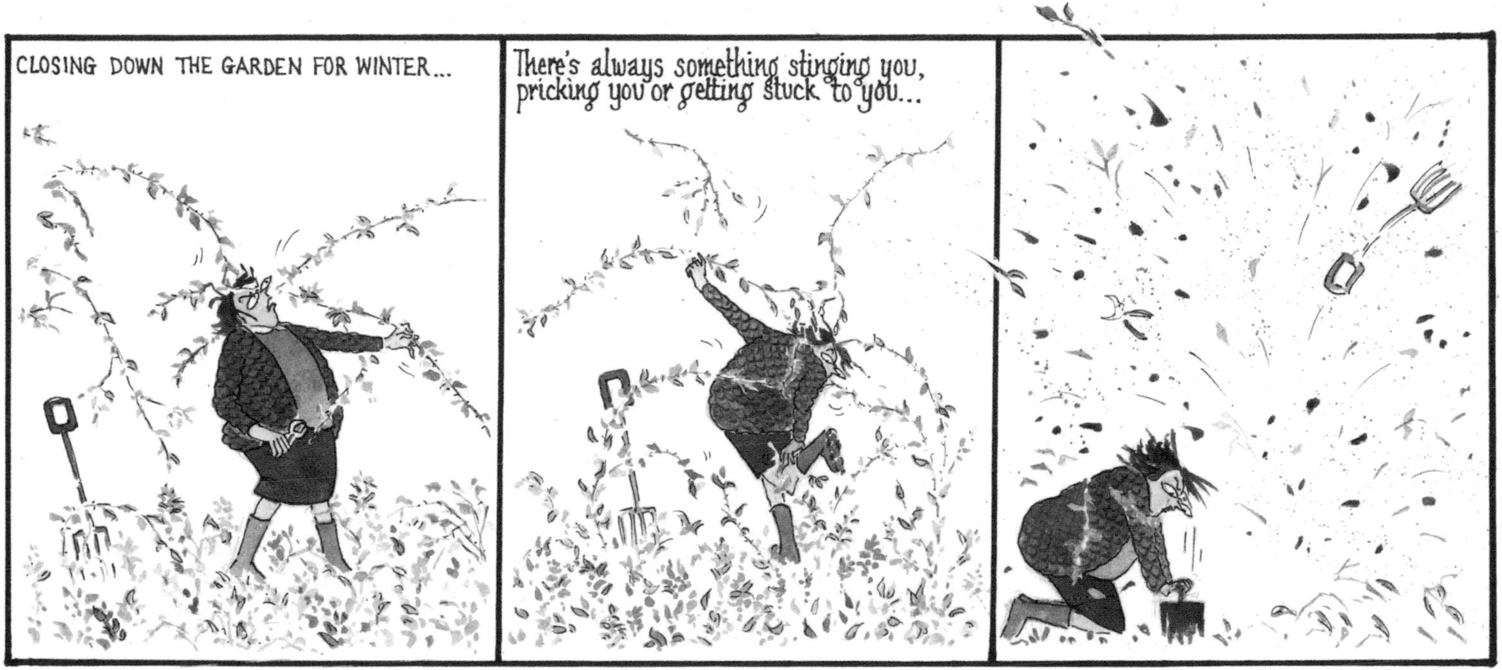
CLOSING DOWN THE GARDEN FOR WINTER...
There's always something stinging you, pricking you or getting stuck to you...

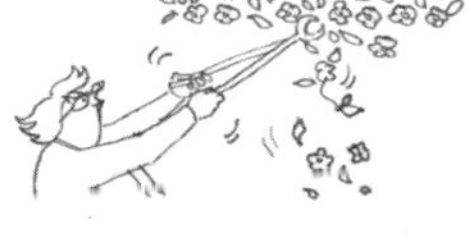

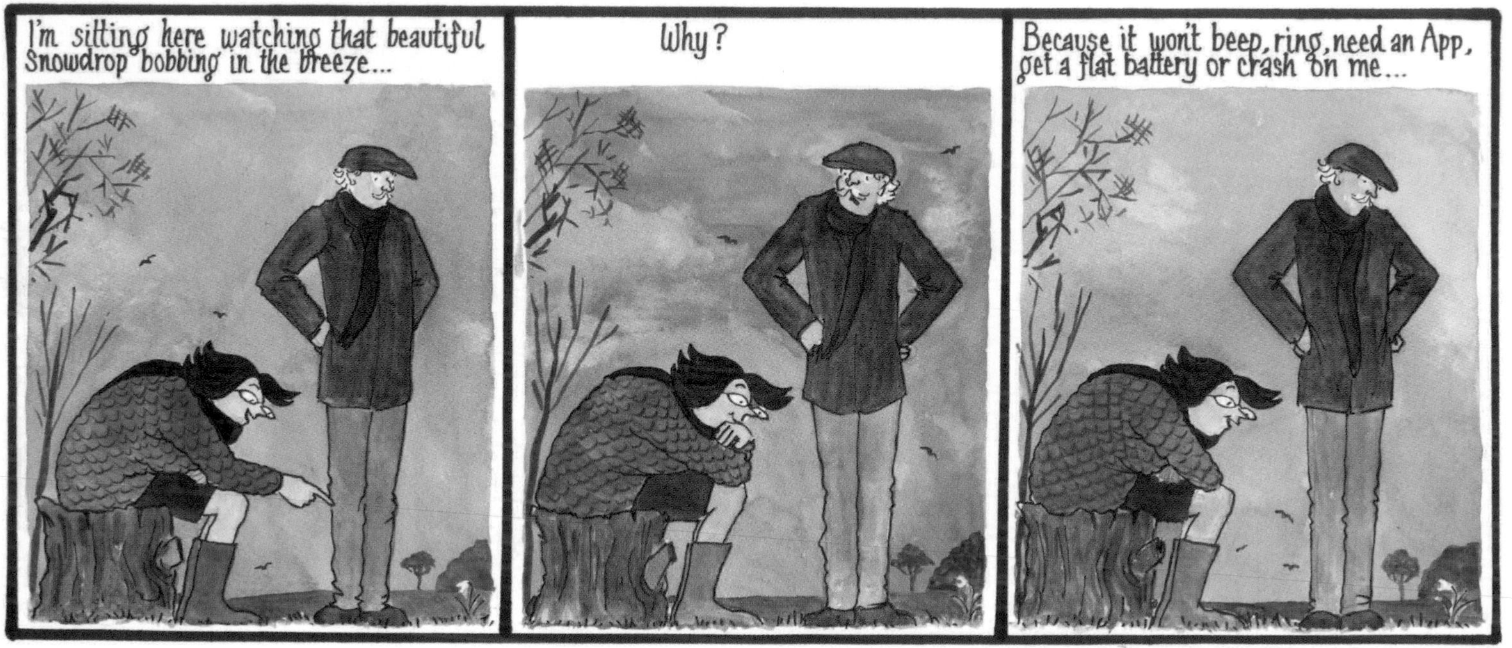
I'm sitting here watching that beautiful snowdrop bobbing in the breeze...
Why?
Because it won't beep, ring, need an App, get a flat battery or crash on me...

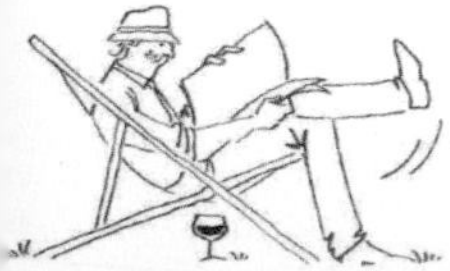

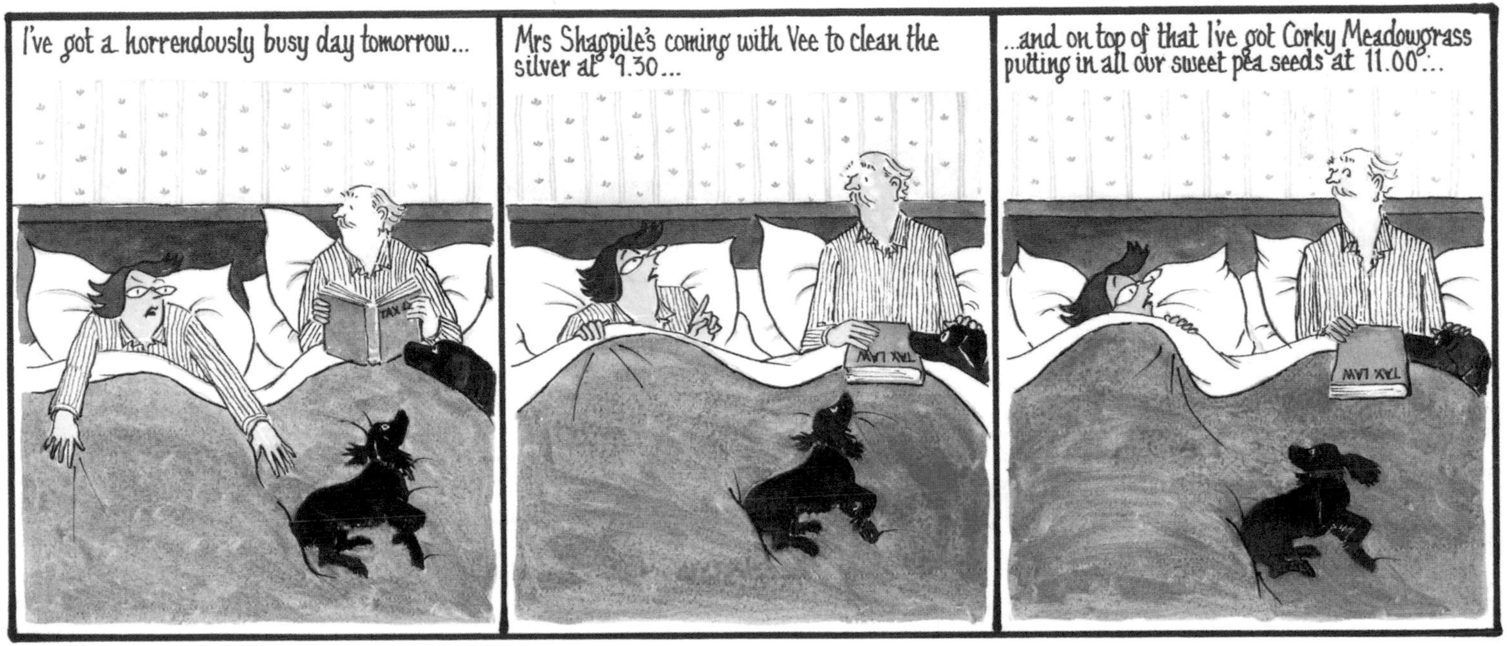
I've got a horrendously busy day tomorrow...
Mrs Shagpile's coming with Vee to clean the silver at 9.30...
TAX LAW
...and on top of that I've got Corky Meadowgrass putting in all our sweet pea seeds at 11.00...
TAX LAW

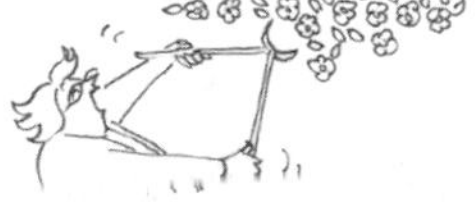

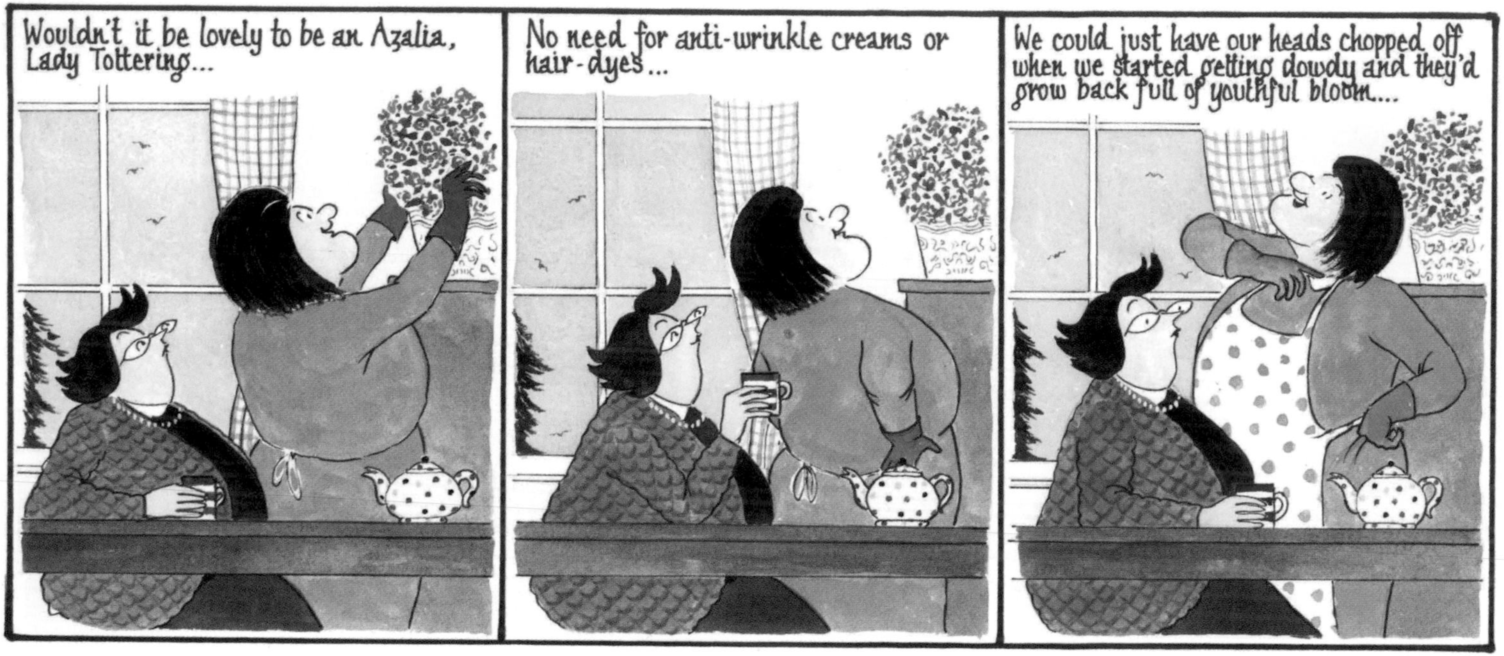

Wouldn't it be lovely to be an Azalia, Lady Tottering...
No need for anti-wrinkle creams or hair-dyes...
We could just have our heads chopped off when we started getting dowdy and they'd grow back full of youthful bloom....

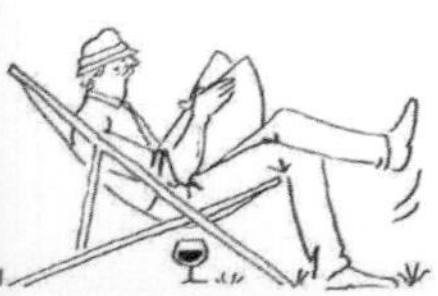

Scribble and I have raked all the leaves up. We're heading in for our treats... A large gin and tonic and a Boneo, please...

Don't look back... Just... Don't look!

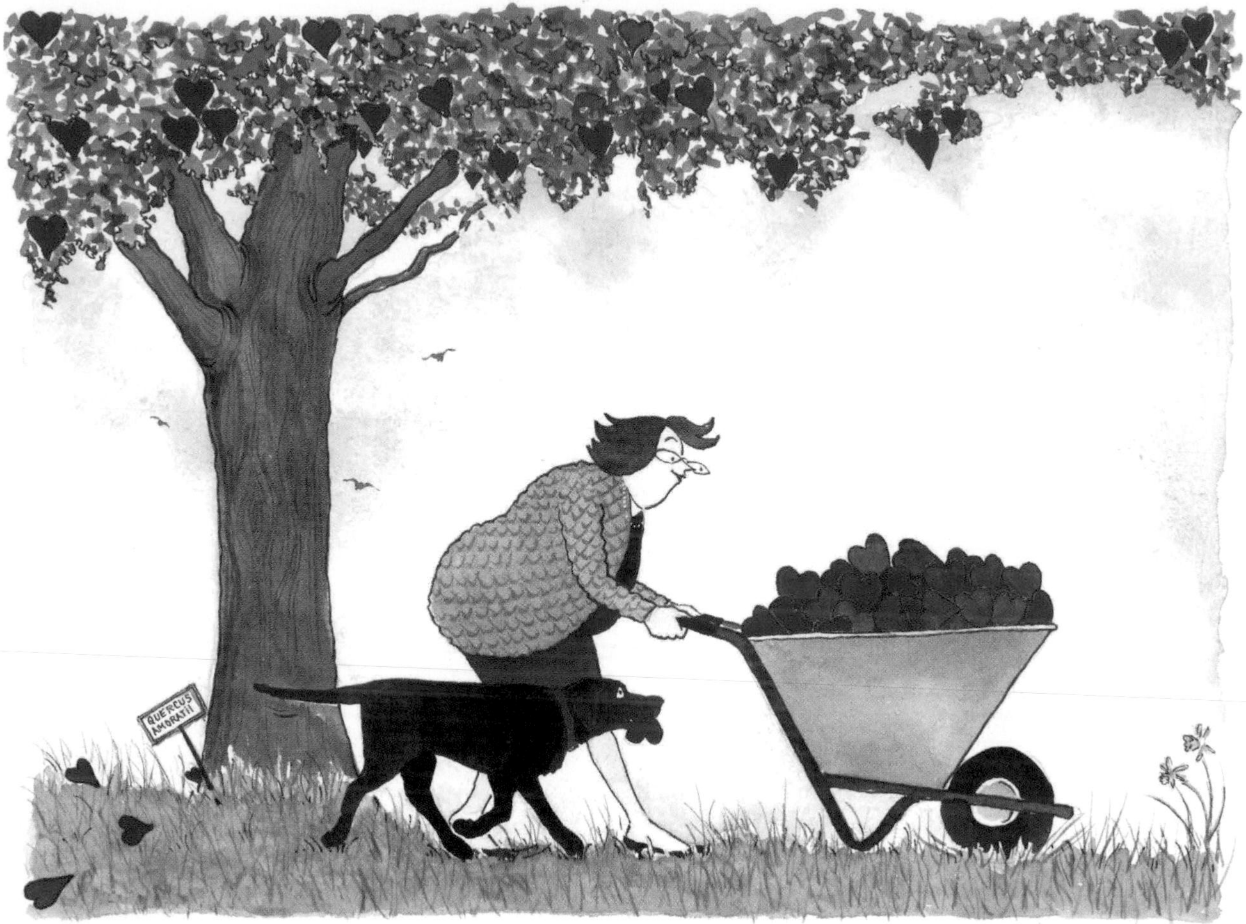
QUERCUS AMORATII

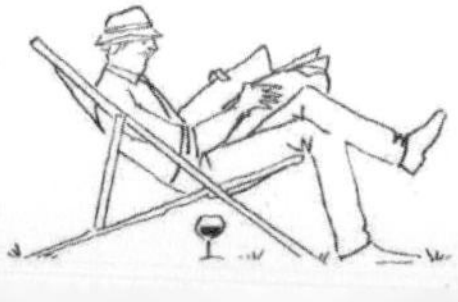

Heading for the best spot in the garden for a family sun-downer...

I like the Provençal lawn irrigation system...

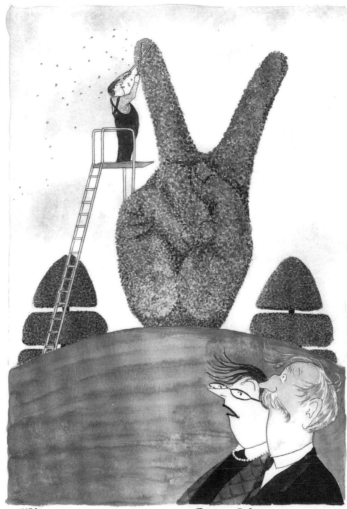

"I'M NOT SURE THAT GIVING Corky Meadowgrass
A FREE HAND IS SUCH A GOOD IDEA, Daffy..."

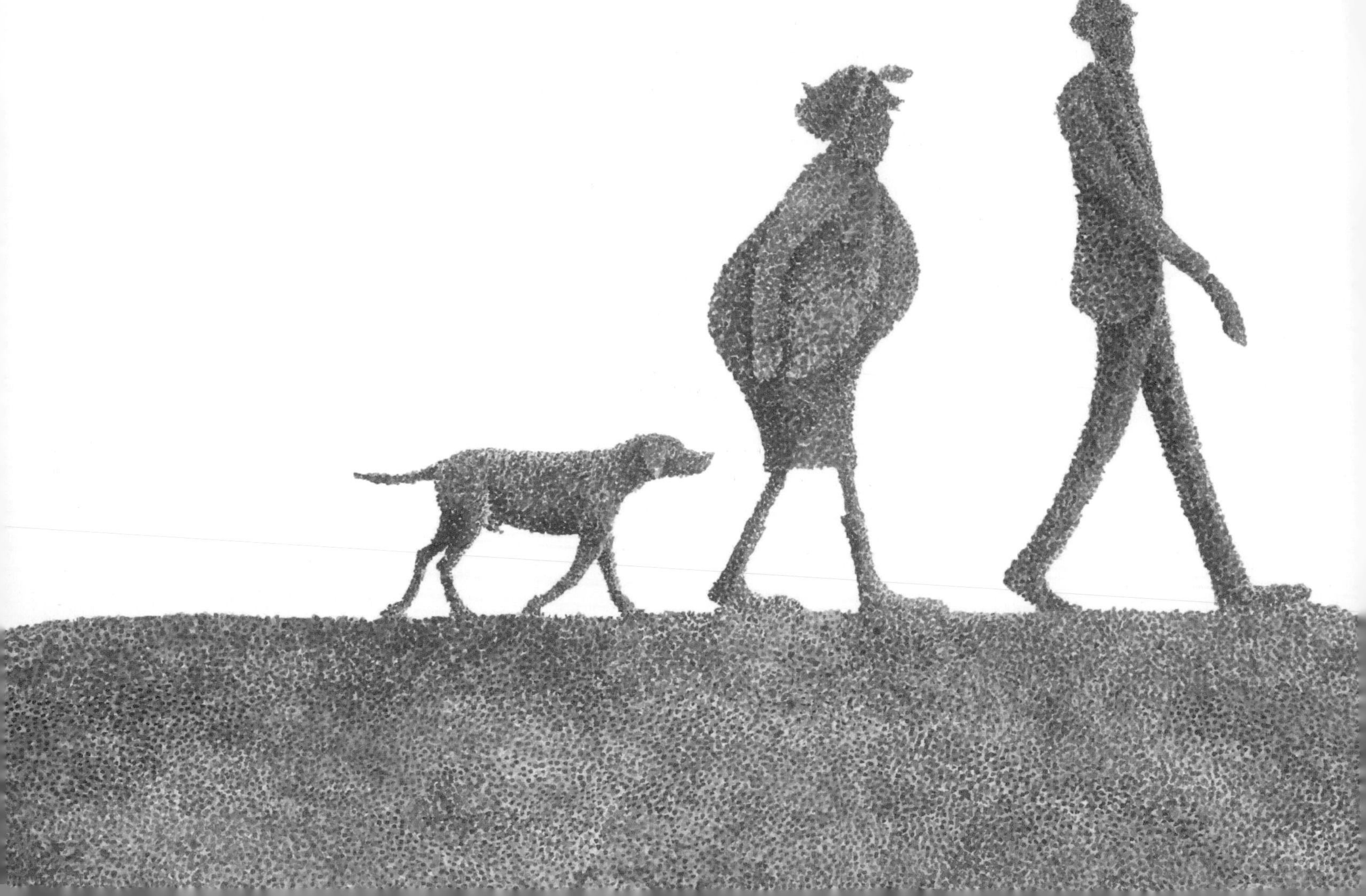

TOTTERING BRAND

Cartoonist ANNIE TEMPEST's famous world of Tottering-by-Gently®, which appears weekly in *Country Life* magazine, has spawned a wonderful range of original and stylish gifts. Her main characters, Dicky and Daffy, and their extended family living at Tottering Hall, the crumbling stately pile, provide the essence for her wickedly observant humour covering all aspects of the human condition.

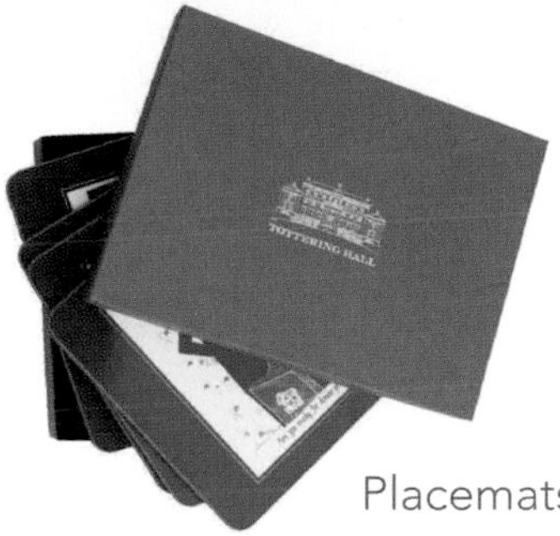

TOTTERING HALL

Placemats

The Tottering range of gifts is suitable for everyone with a sense of fun, including:

- Signed numbered edition prints
- Digital prints on demand (any ANNIE TEMPEST image can be produced as a print)
- Books
- Greeting cards
- Postcards
- Diaries
- Coasters,
- Tablemats,
- Trays,
- Mugs,
- Tins,
- Tea towels,
- Hob covers

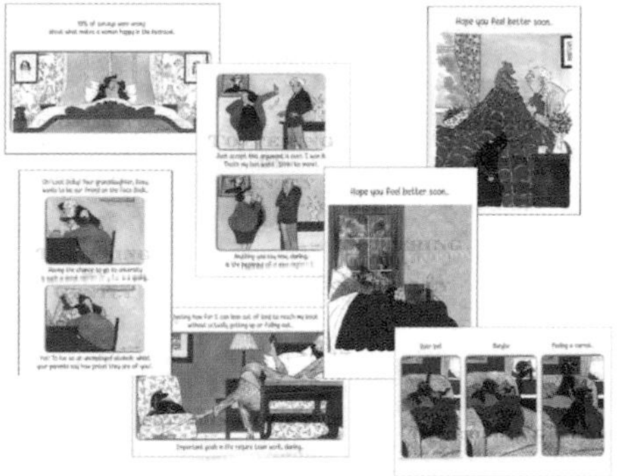

Hope you feel better soon.

Cards and stationery

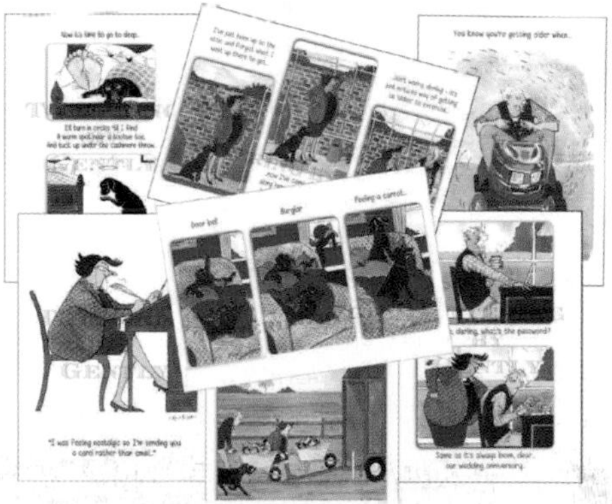

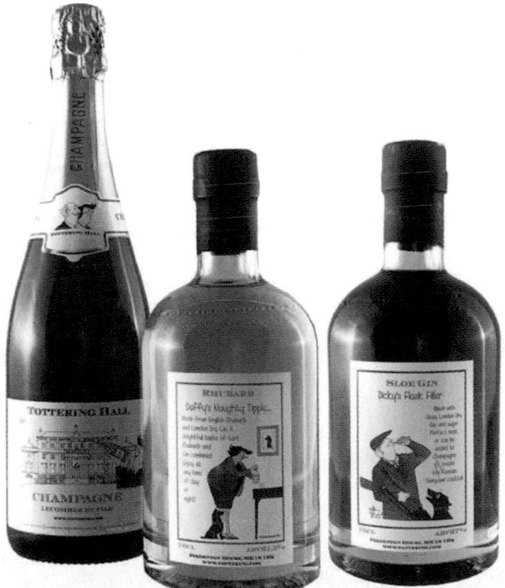

CHAMPAGNE
TOTTERING HALL
RHUBARB
SLOE GIN

... and many other gift ideas. We even have our own brand of Tottering-by-Gently® champagne, wines and gin!

Order from our secure website
at www.tottering.com

or to buy original Annie Tempest artwork visit
www.osheagallery.com

Plus lots more!

All available to order online at
www.tottering.com

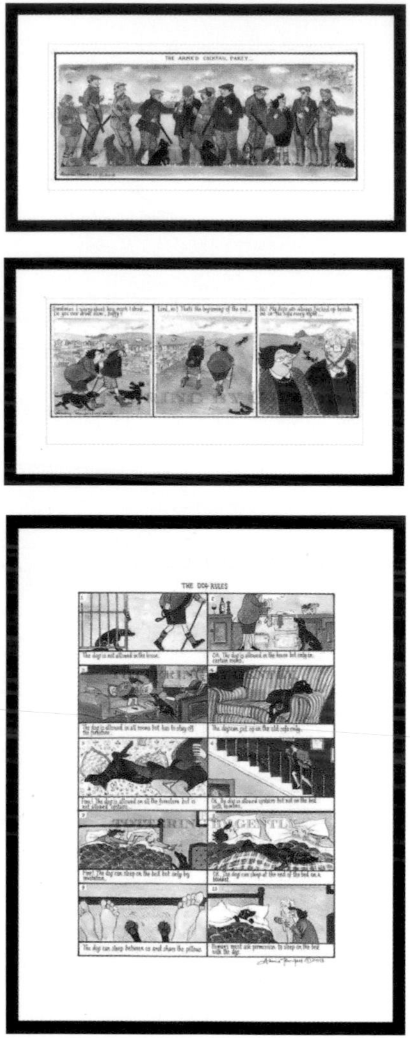

Framed prints

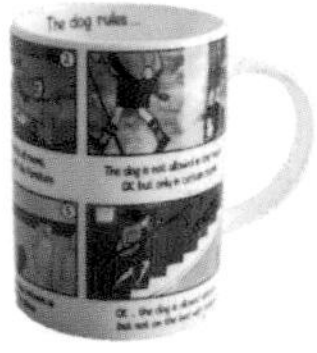

Mugs

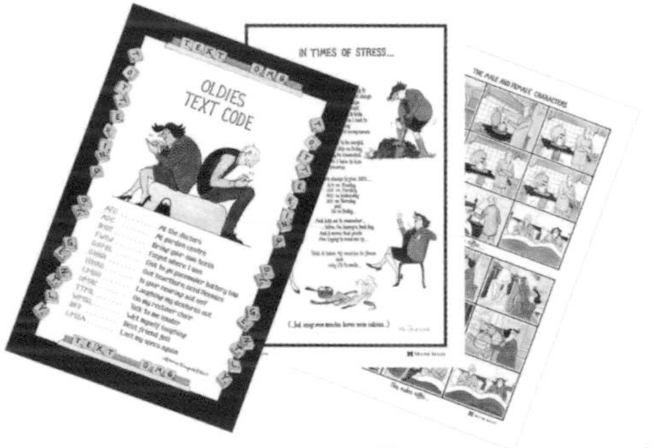
OLDIES TEXT CODE
IN TIMES OF STRESS...

Cotton tea towels

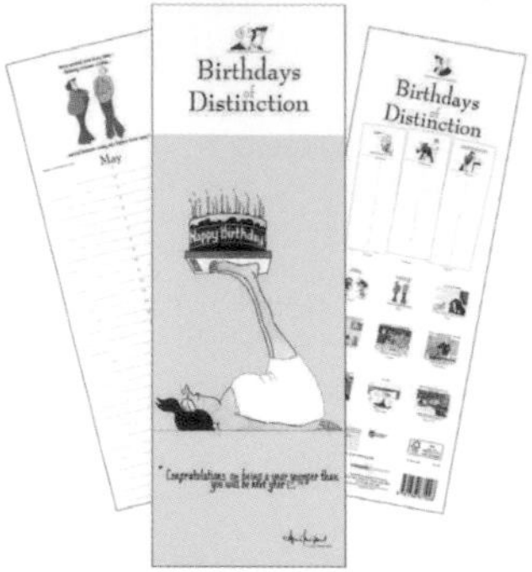
Birthdays of Distinction
Birthdays of Distinction

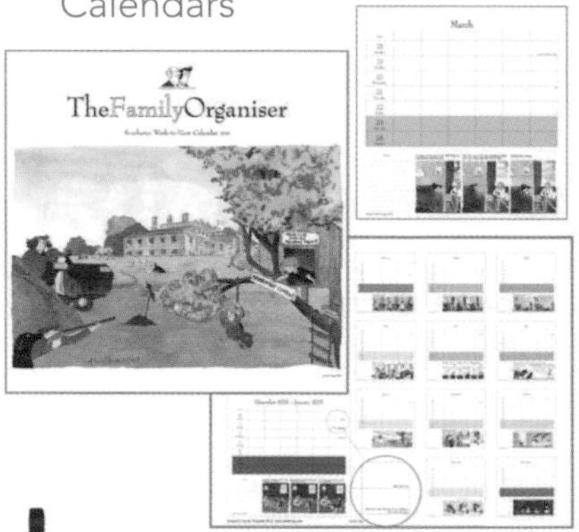
The Family Organiser

Calendars

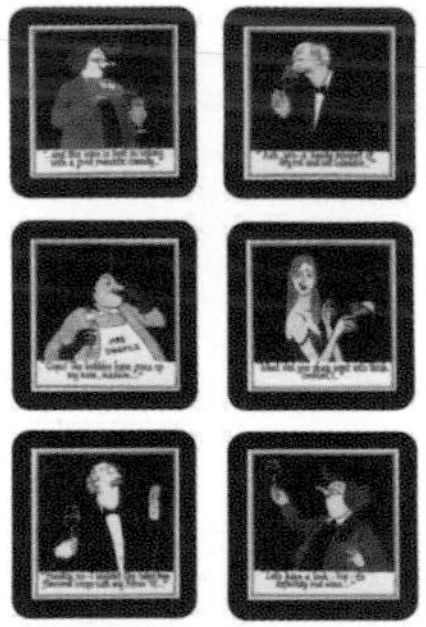

Coasters

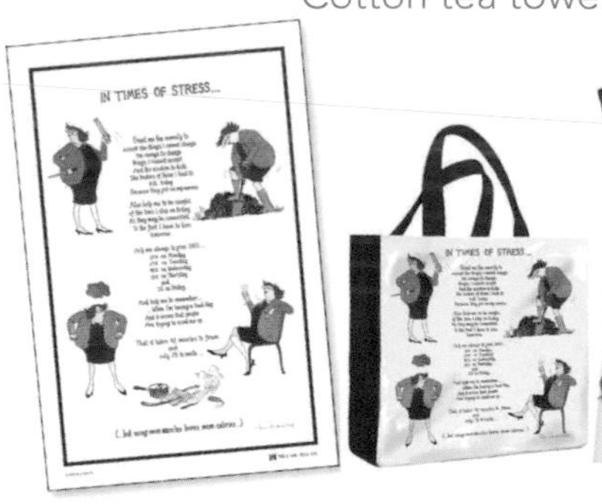
IN TIMES OF STRESS...

PVC mini gusset bags

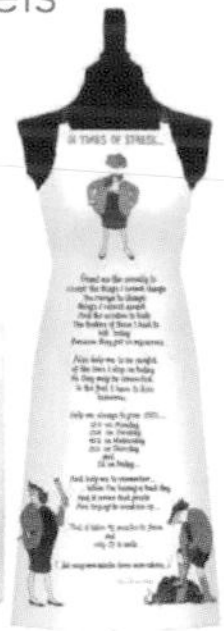

Cotton apron

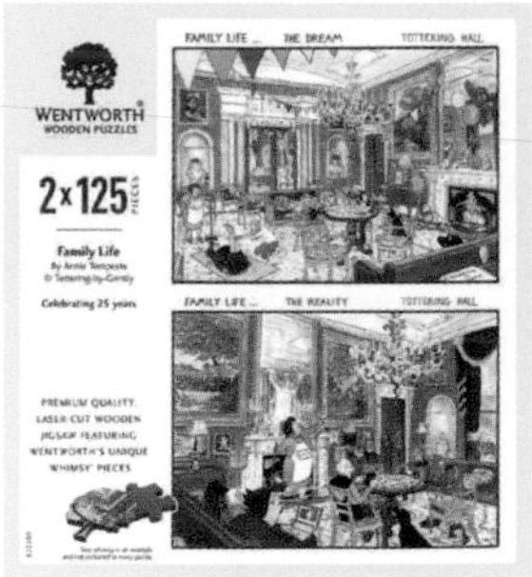
WENTWORTH
WOODEN PUZZLES
2×125
Family Life
Celebrating 25 years

Puzzles

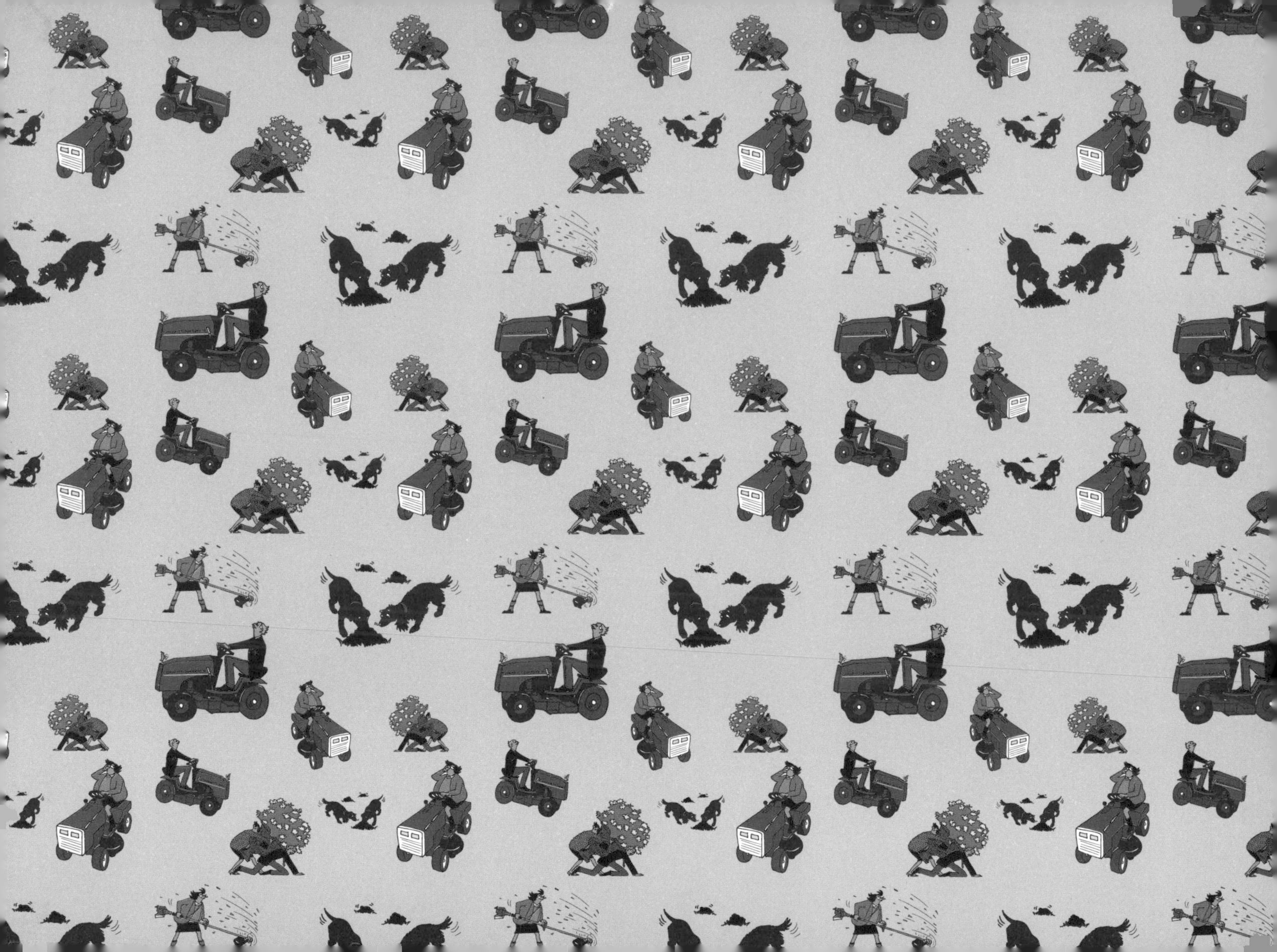